TWELVE BAD MEN

LOUIS XI
1423–1483

TWELVE BAD MEN

By SIDNEY DARK

With Portraits by
MABEL PUGH

Essay Index Reprint Series

 BOOKS FOR LIBRARIES PRESS
FREEPORT, NEW YORK

First Published 1929
Reprinted 1968

LIBRARY OF CONGRESS CATALOG CARD NUMBER:
68-54343

PRINTED IN THE UNITED STATES OF AMERICA

CONTENTS

CONTENTS

LOUIS XI

LOUIS XI

FOR the unlearned, the past lives, not as it was, but as the writers of romance have imagined it. The real Louis XI was not the Louis XI of Walter Scott. The real Richelieu was not the Richelieu of Dumas. And historians are, at times, as unreliable as novelists. The real Elizabeth was certainly not the Elizabeth of Froude, or the real William III the William of Macaulay.

Louis XI of France has been particularly unlucky. We know him best from the famous description by Walter Scott in *Quentin Durward*:

The expression of this man's countenance was partly attractive, and partly forbidding. His strong features, sunk cheeks, and hollow eyes had, nevertheless, an expression of shrewdness and humour congenial to the character of the young adventurer. But then, those same sunken eyes, from under the shroud of thick black eyebrows, had something in them that was at once commanding and sinister. Perhaps this effect was increased by the low fur cap, much depressed on the forehead, and adding to the shade from under which those eyes peeped out; but it is certain that the young stranger had some difficulty to reconcile his looks with the meanness of his appearance in other respects. His cap, in particular, in which all men of any quality displayed either a brooch of gold or of silver, was ornamented with a paltry image of the Virgin, in lead, such as the poorer sort of pilgrims bring from Loretto.

Louis has been damned by that low fur cap with its paltry leaden image of Our Lady. With his love of colour and courage, war and derring-do, Scott could feel nothing but rather pitying contempt for the king who decked himself with lead.

Louis was one of the few realists who have ever sat on a European throne. Romance was to him mere illusion. He cared nothing for glory. He cared nothing for words. It was to him a matter of no importance that Edward IV of England should style himself King of France so long as he was not King of France. Peace at any price, and with or without honour, was the basis of his politics, and he consolidated the power of the French monarchy by the discovery of the fact that the purse is mightier than the sword. He was the first politician of the Manchester school.

His reign was an almost unqualified success. He overcame the most formidable difficulties. He trampled on his prancing enemies. He succeeded in attaining nearly everything which he desired. He won the high praises of his most acute contemporaries, and, although his insistence that his subjects should pay taxes seriously affected his popularity, his services to France were of incalculable value. He has indeed been well called the father of French unity. But posterity cannot forget the leaden Virgin.

Louis was a man of thirty-eight when he succeeded to the throne in 1461. His father, Charles VII, unwillingly compelled by Joan of Arc to the famous journey to Rheims, has been not unfairly drawn by Mr. Bernard Shaw. He was a miserable, weak, sickly prince. He had been made a king by a saint, and he was never more than a shadow of a king except when he was under the influence of a courtesan, the famous Agnes Sorel. Louis was six when his father was crowned, and Mr. Shaw describes him—again probably not unfairly—as a "selfish little beast." He was a secretive, abnormally

intelligent, and extremely precocious child, and
that was certainly lucky for him, since he was only
thirteen when he was married by his father to Margaret of Scotland, who was a year his junior, a princess with her head full of romance, *"parfaite aux
beautés de l'âme et du corps,"* who must have been
repelled by the drab, plain, commonplace boy-hus-
band selected for her, with his cold obstinacy and
his absorbing interest in politics and hunting. The
marriage was as unhappy as it promised to be,
though Louis seems to have shown his wife quite
as much consideration and attention as was common at royal courts in the fifteenth century. Margaret died when Louis was twenty-two, and the
hitherto smouldering hostility to his father broke
out into open enmity.

In 1447, Louis left the royal court for the independent government of the Dauphiné, the ancient
province of France that lay between Provence and
Savoy. Father and son never met again. Louis governed the province as he afterwards governed
France. He made friends with the traders, and
patronised the Jewish bankers. He clipped the

claws of the nobles, and he contrived to obtain
three or four times more revenue from the province
than had been collected before. His success made
his father jealous and apprehensive, and, when he
heard of a foreign alliance negotiated with the evident intention of establishing an independent kingdom, Charles marched south with a considerable
army, and in 1456 formally incorporated the
Dauphiné into the French kingdom. Louis fled to
Flanders where he lived, until his father's death,
under the protection of Philip the Good, Duke of
Burgundy, a prince who in his love of pomp and
love of letters anticipated the Renaissance, and
who was in every respect a striking contrast to his
guest, the keen-eyed, cunning young Frenchman
to whom a stab in the back always appeared the
wisest form of warfare. When Charles heard that
his cousin of Burgundy was sheltering his son he
said: "He receives into his house a fox which will
eat his hand." And Commines writes of the effect
on Louis of these years of exile and dependence:
"He was forced to make himself agreeable to those

of whom he had need, and this advantage—no small one—adversity taught him."

Burgundy was the most important of the vassals of the king of France. The duchy was originally confined to the district between the Jura Mountains and the River Saône—afterwards known as Franche-Comté—but Duke Philip's territory included not only a large part of what is now eastern France, but extended, in the north-west, along the valley of the Somme, and included Flanders. The vassalage of this formidable prince to the French King was purely nominal. In effect he was an independent sovereign, and one of the most powerful in Europe. It will be remembered that, in alliance with Henry V, Philip had fought against France, and was largely responsible for the humiliation that culminated in the crowning of Henry VI in Paris as King of France, and that Burgundian soldiers played their part with the English in the martyrdom of St. Joan.

The wars that had ruined France had brought prosperity to Burgundy:

[14]

It is unnecessary to point out to the traveller the boundary at which one passes from the Burgundian suzerainty on to French territory. Hardly have you set foot in the kingdom before the aspect of the country becomes sordid and rough: uncultivated fields, briars, thorns, and brushwood; some few field workers, emaciated and bloodless, covered with rags; in the towns and villages numerous ruins and empty dwellings, and, in those which are inhabited, poor and insufficient furniture, a picture of wretchedness, depression, and servitude; but now behold us under the Burgundian government: everything is flourishing, resplendent, growing; there are numerous towns and fortresses; the population is large, the houses are varied and of splendid appearance, full of fine furnishings; the fields are cultivated, the fences in a good state; the people are well dressed and smiling.

Charles VII rode to Rheims with St. Joan. When Charles died, Louis XI rode to Rheims with Philip the Good. The Duke was escorted by four thousand followers. He and his son blazed with jewels. Their horses were saddled in velvet and garnished with silver bells. By contrast, Louis was a figure of poverty, and his second wife, Charlotte of Savoy, whom he had married against his father's wish, travelled in a borrowed carriage. Philip him-

self crowned the King in Rheims Cathedral; Philip
rode by his side in the progress to Paris; Philip was
the outstanding figure in the entry into the capital.
It was he with his jewels and his ladies who impressed the people. "Here is a man," was the cry
of the dazzled Paris crowds who hardly noticed
mean little Louis taking a second place without a
protest, but already thinking and plotting. He had
no desire to deck himself in satin and brocades. He
had no care for costly tapestries and ornaments.
But, as he watched his great rival, it occurred to
him that, since men wanted these foolish things,
it would be good for France that they should be
manufactured within her borders and not imported
from abroad. And he began his reign with the encouragement of trade which made him the *bourgeois* king in a far truer sense than Louis Philippe
with his umbrella. He started the looms at Lyons.
He encouraged weavers and dyers, and he engaged
foreign experts to teach his people handicrafts.

The Duke of Burgundy was not the only vassal
of France powerful enough to challenge the authority of the throne. The Duke of Brittany was

practically independent and made his own treaties with the King of England. Two other great western provinces, Guienne and Normandy, were more than half English in sympathy. The Duke of Anjou, the Duke of Nemours, and a dozen others gave no greater recognition to the King than that he was *primus inter pares*. Throughout his reign, Louis's determined policy was to break the power of these great nobles and to compel them to a real and not to a nominal obedience to the King. By plot, by treachery, and by bribery he succeeded, and when he died, twenty-two years afterwards, Brittany alone still possessed a modified independence.

Edward IV ascended the throne of England in the same year as Louis was crowned King of France. There is a striking similarity between the characters of the two sovereigns, although Edward had more respect for the trappings of his craft. Both men were modern in their revolt against mediæval tradition. Both were realists. Both had the instinct of the trader. But the position of Louis was infinitely more difficult. The power of the feudal barons in England had been destroyed by the Wars of the Roses. Possessing a greater security, Edward was able to trade with Louis on more favourable terms, and generally he had the best of the bargains. In the early days of his reign, Louis was threatened with uncomfortable trouble with Edward. That redoubtable lady, Margaret, widow of Henry VI, in her old age the "hateful withered hag" of Shakespeare's *King Richard III,* had fled to France, after the battle of Towton and the final victory of the House of York, and demanded the aid of her kinsman. The French King wrote her polite letters and arranged a great reception for her when she entered Rouen, but he was anxious not to compromise himself and contrived not to meet the exiled queen. Monarchs in exile are always a nuisance to their protectors.

By the Treaty of Arras in 1435, Charles VII had ceded to the Duke of Burgundy certain towns on the Somme which the Duke agreed to return on the payment of four hundred thousand *écus d'or,* and it was one of the first objects of Louis to raise this large sum of money and redeem the towns. By the autumn of 1463 he had collected half the sum, and an appeal to the French cities to find the remainder met with a prompt response. The Duke of Burgundy was astounded and not too pleased when the redemption money was forthcoming. It was amazing to his magnificence that a king who could not afford to buy a new hat could produce four hundred thousand *écus d'or*, and the Duke's heir, afterwards to reign as Charles the Bold, was furious that his father had accepted payment, and for a while had lost the mastery of the Somme valley.

Shortly after the redemption of Amiens, Abbeville, Peronne, and the other towns which to us have tragic and vivid associations, Louis, fearing trouble and hoping much from smooth words, called a council of his truculent vassals. It must have been an extraordinarily interesting and picturesque meeting. The Duke of Burgundy was too old and ill to go himself, but he was represented. The King's brother, the Duke of Berry, soon to be exceedingly troublesome, was there, and there also were two fascinating figures, relics of the France of the Troubadours, soon to pass away in a century of realism and common sense—Réné of Sicily, that perfect figure of romance, and Charles of Orleans, who had beguiled a long imprisonment in England with the writing of rondels. He had celebrated his return from exile by holding a court of poets in his capital of Blois, with Villon among his guests, and his favourite pastime was to float down the Loire on a gorgeous barge, playing chess in the pavilion. Both Réné and Charles were old men, and they must have seemed very foolish old men to the practical King.

The princes promised to serve the King against the world, but a few months afterwards most of them were in arms against him. He was first deserted by his brother, the Duke of Berry, and it was characteristic of Louis that he announced the perfidy, not to the nobles, but to the burgesses of his cities, begging that they, at least, would remain faithful. But the burgesses were even more *bourgeois* than the King, and in the struggle that followed they remained strictly neutral. Louis met danger with subtle energy. He showed considerable knowledge of military strategy, and he was tireless in the endeavour to buy off at least some of the nobles allied against him. The country was laid bare, and there was a return to the horrors of the days when France was ravaged by the English. His enemies were too strong for him, and Louis was forced to sign a treaty which appeared to give them everything that they demanded, including the return to Burgundy of the towns recently bought back at so heavy a price. The King accepted defeat with patience, and he behaved to his triumphant foes with a courtesy which implied uncomfortable menace.

France was horrified at the concessions. The timid burghers began to repent their neutrality, and for the first time in the history of France there were signs of real national and patriotic feeling, which had considerable political result. In particular there was strong popular protest against the cession of the province of Normandy to the Duke of Berry. Louis undoubtedly appreciated this public feeling, and did not underestimate its value. No sooner, indeed, had he conceded than he plotted to recover, and in a few months Normandy was re-united to the crown of France.

But further humiliation had to be endured. Louis was lured to Peronne in the year 1468, practically made prisoner by Charles of Burgundy, who had succeeded his father in the year before, and compelled to march with the Burgundian army against Liège, a city traditionally friendly to France. He did his best to save the city, famous for its obstinate courage and doomed to destruction by the fiery Charles. But his pleas were disregarded, and he himself was grossly insulted. He bore it all apparently with patience and indifference. But, when he was permitted to return to Paris, he was furiously angry with the Parisians for teaching their magpies and jackdaws to cry "Peronne," as the King passed, and he did not forget the men responsible for his last and most bitter humiliation. His Minister, the Cardinal Balue, had been guilty of treachery. He and his accomplice, the Bishop of Verdun, were given a fair and impartial trial. They were found guilty, and were both imprisoned in a cage of iron eight feet square, which the Bishop of

Verdun himself had invented. The punishment is often cited as an instance of Louis's cruelty, but, though the imprisonment must have been uncomfortable, the cages were fixed in upper rooms, and they were more endurable than the slimy dungeons in which prisoners were frequently confined. It is recorded that Cardinal and Bishop "passed eleven years in tranquil retirement undisturbed by tumults, unharassed by the temptations of the world."

It must have appeared to the well-informed and intelligent observer of public affairs in 1468 that Charles of Burgundy, the picturesque, courageous adventurer, was destined to become the dominant power of southern and western Europe, and that Louis of France was little more than a puppet king. But nine years afterwards, Charles was dead, the King's brother was dead, others of his enemies had either been suppressed or bribed into subjection, and Louis was King of a united France. The nine years were a period of insistent anxiety. Charles made a bold attempt to recover the towns of Picardy, and was driven from the walls of Beauvais only to turn south to ravage Normandy. Edward IV, supported by the Burgundian, had landed with an army at Calais, and had been prevented from advancing into France by the King's ruthless laying waste of his own province, burning down farm-houses and growing crops. As always, it was the people who paid for the ambitious dreams of princes.

The Duke Charles learned at last that the power of the little lean man, with the leaden image of Our Lady in his hat, was not to be destroyed by the most gallant force of arms. He was compelled to abandon the dream of reigning in France, but he did not cease to dream dreams. His dreams indeed became more grandiose. He imagined a great king-dom stretching from Flanders to the Mediterranean which should acknowledge him as over-lord. It was on the hard rock of Swiss determination that his ambition was broken. He was killed in a battle out-side the walls of Nancy, and the Duchy of Bur-gundy reverted to the French Crown, though Flan-ders went, through the marriage of Charles's daughter, to the Emperor, to descend from him, in the course of less than a century, to Philip of Spain, and to provide the scene of one of the great dramas of history. It is said that Louis was vastly disappointed at losing Flanders. As a matter of fact, there is no evidence that he ever desired to rule outside the borders of France. His successors, Charles VIII and Louis XII, ruined themselves by ridiculous attempts to establish a sort of French suzerainty in Italy. But Louis XI had none of the ambitions of a conqueror. He could see beyond the end of his nose, but he certainly never could see beyond the borders of his country, and his political ambition was limited by the desire to create a united France, actually subject to the rule of a central monarchy and not the prey of contending princes, half a dozen of whom were alone strong enough to oppose the King, and who, in temporary alliance, could always successfully challenge the royal authority.

It is not necessary for me to trace in detail the plottings, the manœuvrings, and the bribings by which this royal authority was established, not again to be challenged until the rise of the power of the House of Guise and the distraction caused by the Reformation which temporarily destroyed the unity of France, as it has permanently destroyed the unity of Europe.

Louis XI has been called the royal Uriah Heep. He pretended to a humility that was always very dangerous. But he was entirely sincere in his contempt of pomp and circumstances. He honestly preferred the society of his barber to the company of princes, and probably the preference showed admirable judgment. He was single-minded in his patriotic ambition, and his services to his country were of incalculable value. But as some men are great in their vices, so Louis was mean in his virtues. He was a considerate husband, and his second wife, a simple and retiring princess, had a much pleasanter life than that which fell to most great ladies of her age. He had a deep affection for his elder daughter and for his sister, though he treated his younger daughter, the hunchback Jeanne, with neglectful inconsiderateness. He took immense pains to secure a peaceful succession for his son. This much may be said for him, but the man was bloodless. He had no love for any single human being and certainly not for himself, and, while he may be applauded for his dislike of war, it cannot be forgotten that his policy of conquest by bribery was as costly as the more picturesque method of conquest by force of arms, and, while the laying waste of Picardy to prevent the advance of an English army may be justified on the score of political expediency, it shows the same disregard for the interest of the common folk as was habitually shown by Charles of Burgundy and the other conquering generals of the age.

In order to raise the immense revenue necessary for his political purpose, Louis encouraged trade, and remained the constant friend of the trading classes. But the *bourgeoisie* is never grateful, and the traders of Lyons and Marseilles, however much they owed Louis, resented the high taxation that he imposed quite as much as the great princes resented their subjection to his will. And while he was as benevolent as expediency would permit to the middle classes, he constantly ground the faces of the poor. During his reign the people of France lost

[27]

a great deal of what was most beneficent in the circumstances of the middle ages. For the first time the craftsman found himself shut out from the guilds of his craft, while the countryman starved that the taxes might be paid. Moreover, Louis cared nothing for law and justice, although, when it served his occasion and when he was assured of the verdict, he might make an effective pretence that a fair trial was given to his enemies. The King made the laws, the King's creatures administered them. Burgundy lost heavily by its incorporation with France. De Tocqueville says: "Louis XI destroyed all the popular and democratic character of the towns, and kept their government in a small number of families attached to his reform and bound to his power by immense benefits."

Politically, Louis may be said to have anticipated Pitt. All the world was in his pay. When Edward IV was intriguing with the Duke of Burgundy, the English Ministers were receiving heavy bribes from the French King, and Edward, who was as shrewd as Louis, knew all about it and was glad that his brother should pay his servants. It is impossible not to realise the greatness of the King's achievement, and it is equally impossible not to be moved to a measure of contempt by the means that he employed. Even the dullest of us is enslaved by the conventions of romance. We may see something rather fine in slaying to conquer. We are unable to see anything that is not entirely hateful in paying to conquer. But the shrewdest, the best informed, and the most honest of the King's contemporaries took another view. The chronicler, Philippe de Commines, was a man of the highest probity. "One feels," wrote Sainte-Beuve, "that he would not lie even to increase our admiration for the hero whom he desires to make us love." And Commines asserts of Louis that he never saw a better prince.

Certainly Louis was the most laborious of administrators. He was a prolific letter writer, and his cor-respondents included the burgesses of his towns as well as princes and kings. He was among the first of the moderns. He established a postal service as part of the policy of encouraging trade. He could on occasion, and when policy so dictated, be as

[29]

magnanimous as he could on other occasions be cruel. He lived at the beginning of the Renaissance, but he was untouched by its luxury or its dreams. While he was content with his leaden Virgin, Lorenzo de Medici was reigning in Florence with his court of poets and painters. Louis was, however, keenly interested in the art of printing, and, under his encouragement, printing presses were set up in a dozen French towns in the last decade of his reign. He introduced organs into churches. He encouraged the progress of surgery, and it is characteristic of him that, while he was a patron of many churches, it was the building of *hôtels de ville* that distinguishes his reign. If he cannot be called the father of his people, he was certainly a City Father.

Louis never despaired in adversity, and he never exaggerated prosperity. He was cold, detached, abnormal, and, despite the magnitude of his achievements, from the point of view of the common natural man who laughs and loves and blunders and repents, Louis XI was detestable. The picturesque sinner is easily forgiven. The sins of the mean sinner are inevitably exaggerated. And

Louis knew that he was a sinner. Of the reality of his religion there can be no question. His piety was certainly not hypocrisy. He built shrines and went on pilgrimage. He spent hours in prayer. He gave costly gifts to the Church. He played a large part in popularising the Angelus, that most touching and beautiful acknowledgment of the interest of Our Lady in the men and women for whom her Son died. Louis knew that he was a sinner and so he invoked the aid of the saints.

The truth is that the plotter, mean and cowardly as he often is and hateful with his constant pretence of humility, is nevertheless generally more than a match for the swash-buckler, and, in all probability, he is far less a public nuisance. With his poet's yearning for poetic justice, Dickens makes the end of his Uriah Heep poor and miserable. But Uriah Heep in real life often dies in Park Lane. It is quite common for the mean to inherit the earth. Their tragedy is that they never enjoy their inheritance. Your swaggering fellow gets immense satisfaction from his successes however ephemeral they may be. He thoroughly enjoys himself. Louis XI never enjoyed himself. Even at the end, when he might have regarded his work with satisfaction, he was obsessed by the fear that under a weaker king much of what he had done for France would be undone.

Louis XI was an extremely capable master of men, with the power of accurately diagnosing the qualities of the persons against whom he was pitted and with whom he had to deal. He was entirely unscrupulous and almost entirely effective. And this at least may be said for him—that, if he were not a hero to his valet, he seems to have been a hero to his barber, poor Oliver le Daim, who, maligned by Scott, was loaded with gifts by his master and was hanged immediately after his master's death.

CESARE BORGIA

CESARE BORGIA
1478–1507

CESARE BORGIA

THE Borgias, says Mrs. H. A. Taylor, in her *Aspects of the Italian Renaissance*, have become "a world myth of evil," and she adds that "a tremendous force of personality is necessary to make a myth." Rodrigo Borgia reigned in Rome as Pope Alexander VI for only eleven years. His son, Cesare, died when he was thirty-two. The scheme for which they had plotted and poisoned—to establish a Borgia dynasty in central Italy—burst like a bladder when Alexander died. Their achievement was negligible, and even their wickedness has been exaggerated. Neither Alexander nor Cesare was as black as he has been painted. And Lucrezia has been scandalously maligned. None the less, there was tremendous personality behind the Borgia myth and a colossal opportunity for the exercise of personality. To the humanists of western Europe, to Erasmus, to Colet, and to Thomas More, the Renaissance, with its revival of learning, was the beginning of a new and happier era in the world's history. They looked forward, and More wrote *Utopia*. To the princes of Renaissance Italy, the Renaissance was a happy reaction; a relief from the intellectual and moral restrictions of the Middle Ages; a return to an unmoral, luxurious, and cultured paganism. The reaction found its most enlightened and attractive figure in Lorenzo de Medici. It had its most revolting consequences in the capital of Christendom. There was a notable moral decadence at the papal court from the middle to the end of the sixteenth century, and, unfortunately for European civilisation and for the Catholic Church, years more were to pass before the beginning of the cleansing of the Counter-Reformation. It was at the time when luxury, self-indulgence, and crafty statesmanship held Italy in thrall that the Borgias—the Bulls—came as emigrants from their native Spain, to be, in plain truth, bulls in the china shop.

It is childish to fasten on to individuals all the responsibility for the world cataclysms that have resulted from a combination of varied circumstances. Louis XV and the Du Barry, for example, were little more than the figureheads of the social, political, and economic complications that made the revolution of 1789 inevitable. None the less, it is conceivable that had Louis XV possessed character and discretion, France might have been saved from the Terror and Europe might have escaped Napoleon. So it is also conceivable that, if the Borgias had remained in Spain, the Catholic Church might have winnowed the Renaissance, taking from it all that was splendid and rejecting all that was base, that the Reformation and the break-up of the European comity might have been avoided and the Counter-Reformation have been unnecessary. But in the great drama of history great opportunities have almost invariably either been used or misused by great personalities.

The Pope Alexander was a far-sighted statesman, an able administrator, and a man who had the courage to disdain the concealment of his vices or the hypocritical pretence to a virtue which he did not possess. Morally, he was no worse than his predecessor Innocent VIII. But his vices were more picturesque. The Pope was genial and laughter-loving, amiable and disinclined to severity except when he was convinced that it was necessary for the security of himself and his family. Then he was relentless, and he would plan the murder of a cardinal with just as much and just as little reluctance as a modern woman dismisses a housemaid. His son, Cesare, was colder, more calculating, and, if Machiavelli is to be believed, more far-sighted. Machiavelli contends that, great as were Cesare's qualities, the circumstances against which he had to contend were too great for any man, although it may be fairly suggested that Napoleon, the greatest of all alien rulers, conquered circumstances infinitely more difficult.

The story of the Borgia family begins with Alonzo, the uncle of Rodrigo, who, after acting as secretary to the King of Aragon, became Bishop of Valencia in 1429, cardinal in 1444, and ascended the papal throne as Calixtus III in 1455, at the age of seventy-seven. Two years before the papal crown was placed upon his head, Constantinople had been captured by the Turks, and it was the not ignoble ambition of the papacy of Calixtus to excite Europe to another Crusade "against the irreconcilable enemies of Christendom," and to re-capture the city of Constantine.

But in the last half of the fifteenth century Europe was in no mood for chivalrous adventure. England was torn by the Wars of the Roses. In France, in the last years of the reign of Charles VII, the King and the great territorial dukes were intriguing for supremacy. Spain had still some years to wait for the reign of Ferdinand and Isabella and the beginning of the prolonged struggle to expel the Moors. Calixtus called, but no one heeded, though his short pontificate was made joyful by the defeat of the Turks by the Hungarian hero, Hunyadi, and the destruction of the Turkish fleet by Cardinal Scarampa. It is odd to read of a cardinal gaining a naval victory, but, if an ecclesiastic must mount the quarter-deck, it is well that he should defeat the enemies of the faith.

Like all the Borgias, Calixtus saw that positions of honour and emolument were bestowed on his relations, and particularly on his favourite nephew,

[39]

Rodrigo. But he himself cared nothing for luxury. While he was Pope it is related that "the Vatican resembled an infirmary where the Pontiff spent the greater part of his time by candlelight in bed, surrounded by nephews and mendicant friars." Calixtus died in 1458, and thirty-four years passed before Rodrigo became Pope. He was then admittedly the father of at least five children, the mother of whom was a Roman woman of the middle class, Catarina Vannozza Catani. His four sons were Pedro Louis, born in 1467; Giovanni, born in 1474; Cesare, born in 1476, and Jofre, born in 1481. His only daughter, Lucrezia, was born in 1480. Rodrigo was certainly an affectionate father, and never made the slightest effort to deny his children. His life from the death of his uncle to the beginning of his own pontificate was extraordinarily difficult. The Vatican was the constant scene of baffling and subtle intrigue. But Rodrigo's absorption in ecclesiastical politics was occasionally varied by amorous adventures which in 1460 brought him stern reproof from Pope Pius II. He was then a man of twenty-nine, remarkable for his good looks and address, and enjoying from one office or another an extremely large income, which he spent with taste and discretion. He was, indeed, distinguished far more for his generosity than for any tendency to that insensate luxury which in a few years was to make Rome notorious and ridiculous.

Pius II was succeeded in 1464 by Paul II, a prelate unaffected by the new learning, almost entirely irreligious, but kindly and unaffected. Sixtus IV reigned from 1471 to 1484. Rodrigo Borgia was largely instrumental in securing his election, and obtained the usual suitable reward. The successor of Sixtus was Innocent VIII, who reigned from 1484 to 1492, an amiable and utterly immoral ecclesiastic who acknowledged his children, established nepotism as a Vatican tradition, and not unnaturally regarded the masterful Rodrigo with a certain suspicion. Rodrigo had been within sight of the tiara before he was thirty, but he was more than sixty when he v s able at last to put it on his head, and then his election was only secured by intrigue and flattery and wholesale bribery.

[41]

His election was certainly welcomed throughout Italy. He had been supported by the Sforzas, and there was public rejoicing in their city of Milan when he was elected. He was supported, too, by the Medicis, and there were similar demonstrations in Florence. The wise men of Venice were glad that a politician of judgment and experience should reign in Rome. His wisdom and justice were praised in Mantua, and Geneva was equally enthusiastic. Perhaps this satisfaction was due to the glimmering of national patriotism, for Alexander's most formidable opponent was the Cardinal Della Rovere, who had been backed by French influence. In the circumstances it was perhaps not unnatural that it was the French Ambassador in Rome who most hotly denounced the simony by which the Borgia became the Pope.

There is, of course, no palliation for the crimes of Alexander VI. But it must be realised that it is the greatness of his figure compared to the insignificance of the other early Renaissance popes that has made him one of the villains of history. His vices were written large for all men to read. Savonarola thundered at the sensual paganism of the Holy Father. Colet shuddered at the wickedness that he found in Rome. The pious groaned and the profane chortled. As has been said, the centre of Christendom was sunk in a sea of pestilence. Smaller men's misdoings could easily be forgotten, but the Borgias were not to be ignored. The evil that they did lived after them, to the world's undoing. The austerity of the Counter-Reformation popes, the good deeds of St. Vincent de Paul and St. Philip Neri, the heroic devotion of St. Ignatius, could not wipe away the memory of the sins of the Borgias, which, more than anything else, made the atmosphere in which the Reformation, with all its exaggerations, was possible. It is to Pope Alexander more than to any other man that the destruction of the unity of Christendom is due. •

Except as his father's accomplice and as the darling object of his father's ambition, Cesare appears a figure of much smaller importance. He murdered capriciously and without scruple, but that was not remarkable in the Italy of his time. The army that he commanded, never with any great success, consisted of only a few thousand men. He was calculating and ambitious, but his ambition never extended beyond the provinces of central Italy. Cesare, indeed, owes his notoriety to Machiavelli, who was twice attached to him as the diplomatic representative of Florence. The two men discussed statecraft and the methods by which the superman could govern his less fortunate fellows. Years afterwards, when Machiavelli was disgraced and exiled, he wrote *The Prince*, basing it on the conversations with Cesare as he remembered them, and presenting the Borgia as the ideal ruler, without scruple, without regard for the moral obligations and restrictions properly imposed on smaller men. *The Prince* had an immense effect on the political development of sixteenth-century Europe. Thomas Cromwell read it, and repeated the Machiavellian maxims to Henry VIII. Both Elizabeth and Henri IV of France were the pupils of the Italian statesman. The Bourbons followed the rule of *The Prince*, and the French Revolution was the result. The influence of Machiavelli is obvious all through the nineteenth century, and Europe is not yet rid of it.

[44]

And it has happened that, thanks to Machiavelli, Cesare Borgia, though his dream of glory was narrow and endured for only a few years, remains a typical figure of villainy.

In 1493, when Cesare was seventeen, and was still only in minor orders, his father created him a cardinal. In 1494 the French made one of their periodic incursions into Italy. In order to reach Naples, the French troops had a long march through the Italian states, and it was on this march that Charles VIII made his league with Savonarola, the friar reformer of Florence. The French King was in Rome in January 1495, and, fearing the treachery of the Borgias, he insisted on taking Cesare with him as a hostage in his march to the south. Charles was weak and worthless, the constant prey of grandiose and vain imaginings, but he was not fool enough to leave himself unprotected against a possible powerful enemy in his rear.

The Pope regarded the French expedition to Naples with at least some benevolence. The Neapolitan King had endeavoured to obtain control of Milan, and, using his influence in this case at least as a good Italian, Alexander had taken measures to defeat the intrigue, and, in the year in which the French troops invaded Neapolitan territory, he married his daughter Lucrezia, then a beautiful child of fourteen, to Giovanni Sforza. The marriage was celebrated at the Vatican on June 12th, and was the occasion of gorgeous festivity. The year before, 1492, is one of the great dates in the world's history, for it was then that Christopher Columbus crossed the Atlantic and landed in the New World.

Lucrezia's marriage was followed by a diplomatic triumph. The King of Naples had hoped that as he was a Spaniard the Spanish King would aid him to obtain his ambitions in Italy. But the Pope bound the Spanish throne to the papacy by the formal grant to Spain, as a result of the enterprise of Columbus, of all lands that should be discovered one hundred miles west of Cape Verde and the Azores.

Cesare must have joined the French army as a hostage shortly after his arrival in Rome. He was at the university of Pisa when his father was elected, and apparently did not come to the Eternal City until late in 1492. He was immediately popu-

[46]

lar. He was always exquisitely dressed, and he had all the accomplishments of his time and of his rank. He was cheerful and light-hearted, handsome and dignified, and, although he was a mere boy, he was already an archbishop with an immense income. In whatever else they may have failed, the Borgias always looked after their own. Twelve new cardinals were created in the autumn of 1493, and one of them was Cesare, who became the Cardinal Deacon of Santa Maria Nuova.

Things went badly with the French expedition from the beginning, and Ferdinand and Isabella of Spain were at last persuaded to threaten France with a war unless the expedition was abandoned. Cesare, weary of the part of hostage, slipped back to Rome in the night, vastly frightening the municipal rulers of that city, who imagined that it would be from the citizens and not from the cardinal that the French would demand reparation.

Led by the Duke of Milan, an anti-French league was formed in the north, which was first joined by Venice, and on Palm Sunday by the Pope, and there was a probability that the French would be cut off from their own frontiers by a powerful Italian army. It was now the turn of Charles to be terrified. He hurried back to Rome, where, however, the Pope was not at home, having taken the occasion to make a diplomatic journey to Perugia. The French King fought the Italians at Fornovo, losing many men and much treasure, but cutting his way through and eventually returning to Paris after one of the most inept military expeditions in history.

The Pope's determination to punish the petty Italian princes who had allied themselves with the French may again be regarded as patriotic statesmanship, and the direction of what was, in effect, little more than a police action was entrusted to his elder son, the Duke of Gandia. The war, such as it was, was short and inconclusive. The papal forces captured eleven towns, but they were defeated by the Orsini and lost a considerable quantity of guns and baggage. This inconclusive result, however, did not prevent the Duke of Gandia from being received in Rome with favour and reward, which was shared by his brother-in-law, Giovanni Sforza, who had accompanied him on the expedition, and Cesare, who could brook no rival in his father's affection, was furiously jealous of his brother and his brother-in-law. Giovanni Sforza scented danger. It was not enough for him to stand on the steps of the papal throne and to receive favours from the hands of the Holy Father. He realised the character of Cesare, and he did not forget that Rome was the home of assassination, and, wise man that he was, he fled in the spring of 1497. The Duke of Gandia remained to receive more dukedoms and lordships from his father, but on the morning of June 15th his body was recovered from the Tiber with the hands tied together and the throat cut. There is not the very smallest doubt that he was murdered by Cesare. The sentimental Alexander was heartbroken and not a little terrified by this first striking evidence of the calculating villainy of Cesare, to whom the crime was not, however, generally accredited until some months after it had taken place. But the Pope appears to have had no illusions, and it is significant that, less than two months after his son was killed, Alexander ordered the search for his murderer to cease, a course of action that certainly suggests that he knew very well who he was and was fearful of the scandal that would follow any attempt at retribution.

Like many another sentimentalist, Alexander passed easily from one emotion to another. His tears were bitter, but his weeping was soon over. As J. A. Symonds has said, "The miserable father rose from the earth, dried his eyes, took food, put from him his remorse, and forgot, together with his grief for Absalom, the reforms which he had promised for the Church." It cannot, however, be denied that he did some service for the Church's reputation when, shortly after the murder of the Duke of Gandia, he released Cesare from his clerical vows and left him free to pursue his dreams of secular rule and glory.

From 1497 Alexander became single-minded in his determination to establish his son as a dominant prince in Italy, the first of a Borgia dynasty that might control a united Italy. Hitherto the Pope, while never ceasing to be a statesman, had been largely swayed by his abnormal lustfulness, turning eagerly from affairs of state to the notorious Vatican entertainments, with their crowds of half-naked courtesans and their luxury, fantastic and not without imagination, never paralleled before except at the Court of the later Roman emperors, and happily never paralleled since. The French troops that had marched through Rome with Charles VIII were astounded at what they saw and heard, and the mediæval soldier was certainly not conspicuously squeamish. Alexander was entirely indifferent to public opinion. For a long time he was as disinclined to persecute Savonarola as his successor Leo X was disinclined to persecute Luther. He was completely unmoral; unconscious, indeed, of any offence; and he combined, quite naturally, a life of amazing self-indulgence with a peculiar devotion, not for a moment to be suspected of insincerity, to the Blessed Mother of God.

There is no reason to believe that after the death of the Duke of Gandia there was any striking change in Alexander's mode of life, but he became obsessed by a devotion to his younger and more brilliant son, whose cold intellect had subjected the passionate impetuosity of his father. Alexander loved all his children—there is not the smallest evidence for the viler stories told of him and his daughter Lucrezia—but Cesare was his idol, and his ambition was to erect his idol on a high altar that all men might worship him.

At the end of 1497, the papal courts annulled the marriage of Lucrezia and Giovanni Sforza, who had lost the Borgia favour when he saved his life by escaping from Rome. The ground for the annulment was that the marriage had never been consummated, and to this both husband and wife took oath, but Lucrezia's protestations of virginity were the topical joke throughout Europe.

In 1498, Charles VIII of France died and was succeeded by Louis XII, who proclaimed himself King of France and the two Sicilies and Duke of Milan. This indication of the determination to pursue the old will-o'-the-wisp of French rule in Italy was an intimation to the Vatican of a possible political intrigue. Cesare was laicised, and it was necessary that his political ambitions should be furthered by the most suitable matrimonial alliance. The immediate business was the consolidation of the Romagna under the papal rule. It was a network of small principalities, and there was a constant fear at Rome that Venice, Milan, and Florence might make an agreement for their partition, for the Pope could have no possible chance of resisting the alliance of the three most powerful Italian city states.

Italian sentiment generally was hostile to the creation of a powerful central state under the immediate authority of Rome, and it was evident that, if the Borgia ambition was to be realised. it could only be by outside help. Nothing could be expected from Spain, bound as she was by dynastic ties to the reigning family in Naples. It was, therefore, the obvious policy to attempt to effect an alliance with the new French King.

Just before Christmas, 1498, Cesare arrived at the French camp at Chinon, gorgeously arrayed with five rubies as large as beans in his cap and jewels round his neck worth thirty thousand ducats, and attended by a glittering suite of Italians and Spaniards. He rode a magnificent horse, shod, so it is said, with solid gold and caparisoned in a cuirass of gold leaves, the work of a great Italian craftsman. The magnificence was a little overdone. The French King was amused more than impressed, but he was as ready to use Cesare as Cesare was to use him. The visit, however, began with a disappointment. Its main intention was to secure the hand of Carlotta of Aragon, daughter of the King of Naples, who was living at the French Court. But the young lady, wise in her generation, would have none of him. "The damsel," it was reported to the Pope, "either out of contrariness or because so induced by others, which is easier to believe, constantly refuses to hear of the wedding." The French King, however, produced a satisfactory substitute in Charlotte d'Albret, the sister of the King of Navarre and a member of the family that was to give the great Henri IV to France. She was seventeen, beautiful and pious. A satisfactory dowry was forthcoming, though the lady's father made a hard bargain, and Cesare was married on May 12th, 1500. Four months later, a French army marched over the Alps, Louis dreaming of Milan and Cesare of the Romagna. Charlotte was left behind in France, and she and her husband were never to meet again.

Meanwhile Alexander, eager to make friends on all sides, had persuaded the rather unwilling King of Naples, who had no stomach for matrimonial alliances with the "bastards of priests," to consent to the marriage of Don Alfonso—himself illegitimate, by the way—and Lucrezia.

The French army marched through northern Italy; town after town surrendered without a blow; and in October the French King, with Cesare by his side, rode into Milan, and at once the Pope issued a Bull depriving the tyrants of the towns of the Romagna of all their rights and privileges. Milan was in French hands. At the moment there was nothing to fear from Florence, and it was not difficult to propitiate Venice, which dared not risk a quarrel with the French. Cesare raised a large loan in Milan. Louis lent him a considerable French contingent, and on November 7th he marched south. He was twenty-four. He had no sort of military experience. He had never even witnessed a battle.

The object of the expedition is easy to defend. So far as the common people of the Romagna were concerned—and no one gave them a thought—they regarded the papal army as deliverers. The rule of the petty tyrants had been cruel and almost intolerable. No change could occur that would not be a change for the better. But, though this was true, the hand of the foreign mercenaries, if not of their leaders, was very heavy, and the conquest of the country entailed the usual murder and pillage. Its one picturesque incident was the capture of Caterina Sforza, a masterful lady, "eager soul but a most cruel virago," who had shut herself in the castle of Forli and who rode with Cesare, in his triumphal entry into Rome, in golden chains.

The year 1500 was the year of Jubilee. Despite the danger of travel through Italy, Rome was crowded with pilgrims. The Church remained great though Churchmen might be depraved. "The Chris-tian religion," it was said, "does not lack the testimony of pious minds, especially in these times of failing faith and depravity of morals." But Rome was as full of criminals as of the pious. Murder was as common in its streets in the sixteenth century as it is in the Chicago of the twentieth. Cesare dominated the city, and again there were subtle removals of possible rivals. His brother-in-law, Alfonso of Aragon, was attacked by assassins on the very steps of St. Peter's. Alfonso had been suspected, perhaps not unfairly, of intriguing with his own family against the Borgias, and he had no doubt that it was by Cesare's orders that he had been attacked. His wounds slowly healed, but resentment remained. Seeing from his window Cesare walking in the Vatican garden, Alfonso seized his bow and shot at him, and the unfortunate prince was promptly murdered in his own room. Lucrezia was heartbroken, and her grief became annoying both to her father and her brother.

At the end of 1500, having enlisted another army, mainly consisting of foreign mercenaries, Cesare completed the conquest of the Romagna, adding to his cities Rimini, Pesaro, and Faienza, and receiving from his father the title of Duke of the Provinces. Cesare now dreamed of a conquest of Florence, but of this the French King would not hear, and the Florentines made a deal with him by taking him into their service at a large yearly salary. He was back again in Rome before mid-summer, being received again with a welcome out of all proportion to his achievements, "as though he had conquered the lands of the infidels and not of devout subjects of the Holy See."

Louis XII had inherited his predecessor's lust for Italian conquest, and in 1500 a treaty was signed by the Kings of France and Aragon partitioning Neapolitan territory as a preliminary to a crusade against the Turks, which neither of them really intended. Cesare was with the French forces that captured Capua and entered Naples, which surrendered without resistance. While fighting was proceeding in the south, Alexander made a progress through the cities of the Romagna, scandalising Christendom by leaving Lucrezia in Rome as his regent, with authority to open letters and command cardinals.

In September, Lucrezia found a third and last

husband in Alfonso, Duke of Ferrara, who was compelled into the alliance by pressure from the French King against his own wishes and those of his father. The marriage was the occasion for more gorgeous festivities, pageants, theatrical performances, banquets, balls, and bull fights. Lucrezia left Rome in the early part of 1502 with a hundred thousand ducats from the papal treasury. With this third marriage there came to Lucrezia years of quiet and peace. She won the heart of her husband and that of his people. Her life was pious and blameless, and she died loved and regretted in 1519.

In 1503 the star of the Borgia was at its height. Cesare had conquered his enemies. The road to a kingdom seemed open to him. Machiavelli, who had been sent to him as ambassador from Florence, was dazzled both by his genius and his wickedness. He has described him as "a man without compassion, rebellious to Christ, a basilisk, a hydra, deserving of the most wretched end." At the same time, he recognised his foresight, his courage, and his talent as an administrator. Machiavelli insisted that the ruler who would rule must necessarily be without scruple or hesitation. The world cannot be governed by a paternoster.

The Frenchman, Gobineau, who anticipated Nietzsche in his admiration of the "blond beast" has put into the mouth of Alexander VI a summary of the Borgia philosophy. The Pope says to his daughter, Lucrezia:

Know then that, for that kind of persons whom fate summons to dominate others, the ordinary rules of life are reversed, and duty becomes quite different. Good and evil are lifted to another, to a higher region, to a different plane. The virtues that may be applauded in an ordinary woman would in you become vices, merely because they would only be sources of error and ruin. Now the great law of this world is not to do this or that, to avoid one thing and run after another; it is to live, to enlarge and develop one's most active and lofty qualities, in such a way that from any sphere we can always hew ourselves out a way to one that is wider, more airy, more elevated. Never forget that. Walk straight on. Do only what pleases you, but only do it, if it likewise serves you. Leave to the small minds, the rabble of the underlings, all slackness and scruple.

Rome was a city of horror and suspicion in the last years of Alexander's papacy. Wealthy cardinals died mysteriously and their possessions were seized by the Pope. Cesare came and went, no man knew when or whither, sleeping in the daytime, plotting at night. "Not in their houses, in their chambers, or their towers were men safe," wrote Egidius of Viterbo; "the law of God and man alike was set at naught; gold, violence, and lust bore undisputed sway." Cesare's mercenaries preyed on the citizens; murders were a commonplace.

The year 1503, the year of triumph, was also the year of disaster. Alexander VI died of tertiary fever—the story that he was poisoned is reasonable enough, but probably untrue—and Cesare himself was too ill to protect his own interests. Enemies, eager for revenge, multiplied round him. Pius III, a very old man, succeeded Alexander for only a few months, to be followed by Giuliano della Rovere, one of the bitterest of the Borgias' enemies, who was to become the masterful Pope Julius II; and Cesare must have known that the game was up. For a few months the Pope treated him with consideration, but he was obliged to surrender his possessions one after the other, and was at length allowed to leave Rome for Naples, where, however, he was arrested in May 1504, by the order of the King of Spain, and sent to Spain, where he was imprisoned for two years.

In the winter of 1506 he escaped from his prison, crossed the Pyrenees, and arrived at the Court of his brother-in-law, the King of Navarre. From there he sent letters to Italy, but Italy would have none of him. He begged the help of the King of France, but the Borgia was now a broken adventurer, only to be abandoned. The end came in February 1507, when he was killed in the endeavour to capture the castle of Viana, at the head of a contingent of his brother-in-law's troops. It was a mean and a proper end.

It is odd, perhaps, that the world which remembers the wickedness of the Borgias in the fifteenth century hardly remembers that the family produced a saint in the century that followed.

CELLINI

BENVENUTO CELLINI
1500–1571

CELLINI

HALF way across the Ponte Vecchio in Florence is a bronze bust of Benvenuto Cellini, greatest of mediæval craftsmen, and to the right of him and to the left, in the shops which have stood on the bridge since the fourteenth century, is a vast accumulation of modern rubbish with a certain leaven of the antique and the artistic. It is in accord with the irony of history that Cellini who, with all his sins, was an artist of fine taste and supreme achievement, should now stand in effigy amidst a very sea of shoddy.

Cellini was born in Florence in 1500, two years after the martyrdom of Savonarola, and three years before the death of Pope Alexander VI and the passing of the power of the Borgias. He was the contemporary of Da Vinci, Raphael, Titian, Michael Angelo, Botticelli, Ariosto, and Palestrina, with some of whom he was familiar. At the time of his birth, Machiavelli still held official position in Flor-

[65]

ence, to which the Medicis were not to return until Cellini was twelve. His father, Giovanni, was an engineer who had been employed by the magnificent Lorenzo, and the well-being of his comparatively humble family was assured with the revival of the fortunes of the Medici, culminating in the election of the Cardinal Giovanni de' Medici as Pope Leo X in 1513.

Leo X was one of the most typical and one of the most attractive of the Renaissance Italian princes. He was created a cardinal when he was thirteen, and he became Pope at the early age of thirty-eight. It would be ridiculous to say that his character was saintly or his tastes ecclesiastic, and Gobineau had ample historical justification for putting into his mouth the words: "I have the greatest distaste for the susceptibilities of the convent and the sacristy." But he was a cultured, kindly gentleman, the patron of great artists, and, whatever his life may have lacked in religious devotion, he was careful of decorum and never provided material for the scandal-monger. It was the tragedy of the life of Pope Leo that, during his pontificate, Luther broke with the Church and initiated the tragedy of the Reformation. The Pope did everything possible to propitiate a man whose ability he recognised, while he did not deny the existence of the abuses which the German monk denounced. The Medicis had suffered sufficiently through the persecution of Savonarola. "Martin Luther," Gobineau makes him say, "will not obtain from my hand the honour of martyrdom." But the times were not propitious for conciliation, though, if Luther could have been persuaded to come to Rome for a personal interview with the Pope, the history of Europe might have been vastly different.

While Leo reigned in Rome, another Medici, the Cardinal Giulio, a nephew of Lorenzo, was the dominant personality in Florence and the patron of the Cellinis. His father was anxious that Benvenuto should be a musician, but the boy hated "that accursed art," and rebellion against his father's determination encouraged the truculence which all through his life was his most obvious characteristic. He and his brother were concerned in a serious altercation in the streets while they were still in their early teens, and the Cardinal advised Giovanni to send Benvenuto to Bologna where he was apprenticed to a goldsmith, while still being compelled to endure a daily music lesson. The next few years were spent partly in Pisa, where he worked for another goldsmith, and partly at home, where he met Torrigiano, the famous sculptor whose work is among the beauties of Westminster Abbey. Cellini describes Torrigiano as "a handsome man of consummate assurance, having the air of a bravo rather than a sculptor." He was attracted by Benvenuto and tried to persuade him to return with him to England, but the young Florentine declined, partly perhaps from resentment of the fact that Torrigiano had had a scuffle with Michael Angelo in which he had broken the great sculptor's nose, for Cellini had a vast appreciation of the work of his elder contemporaries and particularly of Michael Angelo and Leonardo da Vinci.

When he was twenty-three, another violent quarrel in which he nearly killed his opponent with a dagger compelled Cellini to fly from Florence and make his way to Rome, where he arrived shortly after Giulio de' Medici had become Pope with the title of Clement VII. The new Pope was a cultivated man of considerable ability, but far too timid and narrow-visioned successfully to overcome the difficulties of the times. He was bewildered by the Reformation, and his dependence on the good will of the Emperor Charles V compelled him to the hostility to Henry VIII which has had the most profound result in the history of Europe and of the Catholic Church.

Cellini, who was always a man of tremendous industry, obtained employment with a goldsmith, spent part of his leisure copying the masterpieces of Raphael and Michael Angelo, and found time to practise the cornet sufficiently to obtain employment in the papal band. His father's obstinacy thus had its influence in his son's fortune, for it was as a cornet player that he first obtained the notice of the Pope. But very soon Cellini was recognised as a master craftsman, and, ambitious though he was and eager for money, he treated his customers, even when they were influential ecclesiastics, with audacious brusquerie. He had all the not uncommon artist scorn for his patrons, and never in his life attempted to hide it. Even in the Rome of the Renaissance, Cellini must have been conspicuous for his vices, but he always remained the captain of his craftman's soul. Towards the end of 1523 plague broke out in Rome and Cellini was attacked. He went for his convalescence to Civita Vecchia, and during his stay he was attacked by a band of ruffians. His story of how he escaped is one of the many entertaining and obviously lying incidents with which his *Memoirs* are filled.

In 1527 Rome was besieged and captured by a French army under the command of the Constable de Bourbon. Cellini's description of his part in the defence is delightful in its *gasconades*. He was with the defenders on the walls of the city when the order was given to retire as it was impossible successfully to resist the enemy. But Cellini, so he says, retorted: "Since you have brought me hither I am determined to perform some material action." And, levelling his arquebus, he fired into "the thickest crowd of the enemy" and shot the Duc de Bourbon himself.

With the rest of the papal forces, Cellini took refuge in the Castle of St. Angelo, leaving the city to be sacked. Women and children were put to the sword and "the Blessed Sacrament, the relics of the saints, all holy things, were desecrated and scattered about." It was Cellini who saved the castle from falling into the hands of the French by his promptness in himself directing the artillery. "I continued to fire away," he says, "which made some Cardinals and gentlemen bless me and extol my activity to the skies. Emboldened by this I used my utmost exertions; let it suffice that it was I that preserved the castle that morning and by whose means the other bombardiers began to resume their duty." For a month his zeal never flagged. He roughly forbade the Cardinals to come near him, as their scarlet hats attracted the enemy's fire. "By which," he says, "I incurred their enmity and ill will." In the intervals of firing his guns, he took the Pope's jewels from their settings, sewed the stones into the skirts of the Pope's clothes, and melted down the gold, pocketing a reasonable percentage for himself. But this was a mere incident

in his martial career. "My drawing, my elegant
studies, and my taste for music, all vanished before
this butchering business; and if. I were to give a
particular account of all the exploits I performed
in this infernal employment, I should astonish the
world." I have quoted this description of the siege
of the Castle of St. Angelo at some length, since it
is illustrative of Cellini's ingenuous boastings. In
all the many things at which he tried his hand he
was always, from his own point of view, entirely
successful.

After peace was signed, Cellini went back to
Florence, where he found his father had died of the
plague, and that the Medicis had once more been
driven from the city. Michael Angelo was working
there, and, when the Pope declared war on Florence with the intention of recovering it for his kinsman, Michael Angelo was employed erecting outworks for the defences, and was afterwards compelled to earn the papal pardon by years of work
for which he had little taste. But Cellini was more
astute. Realising that the Pope was likely to be his
most profitable patron, he contrived to return to

Rome, where he was busy producing masterpieces of the goldsmith's craft while Michael Angelo was constructing outworks. But his life was never tranquil for very long. He killed an arquebusier in revenge for killing his brother. He killed a friend of his, with whom he had quarrelled, by striking him on the skull with a stone, and he stabbed an unfortunate who had maddened him by laughing derisively at him. The authorities knew that he was a murderer, and more than suspected that he was a thief. But they also knew that he was a supreme artist, and in sixteenth-century Rome art covered a multitude of sins.

Children of a drab age, only just escaped from the damnable heresy that beauty is the creation of the devil, may well find it hard to understand the men and women of the era that loved beauty as passionately as we love money and ease. In a fine passage in her remarkable book, *Aspect of the Italian Renaissance*, Mrs. R. A. Taylor says:

The gorgeous cups they drank from, the medals that arrogantly declared their love of fame, the platters they ate from, their armour damascened with wonderful devices, their thrones, their doors, their chimney-places, coverlets, cassoni, the temples and pavilions they builded, all lent their zest of beauty to the burning business of dramatic lives. Art was the jewelled tree, that recurrent symbol wistfully indicating the human desire to make imperishable the perfection of a moment. They had drama enough in reality, but, when they rested a little, more drama, processionals, and masquerades must exalt and continue the breathless romance. It is only the devitalised that try to make the hopeless division between life and art, only the fiery and fortunate lovers of adventure who know how to enjoy the miracle whose essence is the stuff of love and hate.

The great painters who "ministered most luxuriously to the pride of the eye" were the chief glory of the Renaissance. But it was perhaps in the achievement of its craftsmen that the love of beauty is most apparent. I again quote Mrs. Taylor:

Supporting and surrounding these great arts of the eye was an infinity of little arts, so that it is difficult to imagine how intricately the setting of life was filled with beautiful work of the hand and the imagination, where now the interstices are stopped with ugly mechanical devices. The churches had their altars, their pulpits, their cantoria, their ciboria, tabernacles, tombs, doors, fonts, balustrades, lamps, candelabra, holy vessels, and sacramental garments, all calling for ingenious craftsmen and great artists. The palaces had hangings, carpets, plate, torch-rests, fireplaces, tarsia-work, reliefs, terracotta, mosaic, their enamels and their majolica. Even pieces of the pavement of the Cortile of Isabella d'Este in the Castello Vecchio are now kept in museums as precious relics. The people had their jewels and embroidered sleeves, the men their swords and helms, the women their golden garlands. Besides the guilds of specialised workers, the artists were ready enough to do anything that participated in the beauty of life, from a statue to a toy, like Cellini; and Leonardo would turn aside to link a curious spiral pattern for woman's sleeve.

Benvenuto Cellini's treatises on the eight branches of "the glorious art of goldsmithing," unfolding the art of *niello,* filigree work, and enamelling, gossiping on how to set a ruby, also about medals, and cardinal's seals, are sharp with zest, lively with wild relish and relief of anecdote concerning papal morses and kingly saltcellars.

It was certainly in an atmosphere "lively with wild relish" and with his own "audacious enjoyable mannerism" that Benvenuto Cellini worked.

The Pope made him Master of the Mint and he designed many beautiful coins. He made clasps and

[75]

chalices, and everything that he made had grace and beauty. He continually haggled, demanding more than was offered him. On occasion he had the hardihood to affront the Pope himself.

At this time he had one of the many love affairs of his life, the details of which, though he recalled them with considerable satisfaction, are nauseous and commonplace. On this occasion, it was with a Sicilian woman called Angelica, whom he found in Naples when he was forced to take refuge there after one of his murders. Angelica was living with her mother, and when Cellini was recalled to Rome he took the daughter with him, and the mother, whose goodwill he bought very cheaply, was left behind. They parted, he records, "Angelica with tears and I with laughter."

Clement VII died in 1534 and was succeeded by Paul III, a wise, austere Pontiff who began the work of the Counter-Reformation. Yet Paul was sufficiently the child of his age to find excuses for Cellini. When protests were made that he was pardoned at the beginning of the new papal reign, the Pope replied, "Men like Benvenuto, unique in their profession, stand above the law." Cellini, however, thought it prudent to leave Rome for a while, and he went first to Florence and thence to Venice. An incident that occurred on the journey illustrates the impish revengefulness of his character. The landlord of an inn, where he and his friends put up, prudently demanded payment in advance. Cellini protested, but was compelled to pay. I quote what followed from the *Memoirs*:

We had very fine new beds, with everything else new, and in the utmost elegance. Notwithstanding all this I never closed my eyes the whole night, being entirely engaged in meditating revenge for the insolent treatment of our landlord. Now it came into my head to set the house on fire, and now to kill four good horses which the fellow had in his stable. I thought it was no difficult matter to put either design into execution, but did not see how I could easily secure my own escape and that of my fellow-travellers afterwards.

At last I resolved to put our luggage into the ferry, and requesting my companions to go on board, I fastened the horses to the rope that drew the vessel, desiring my friends not to move till my return, because I had left a pair of slippers in the room where I lay. This being settled, I went back to the inn, and inquired for the landlord, who told me that he had nothing to say to us,

and that we might all go to the devil. There happened
to be a little stable-boy in the inn, who appeared quite
drowsy. He told me that his master would not stir a
foot for the Pope himself, and asked me to give him
something to drink my health; so I gave him some small
Venetian coin, and desired him to stay awhile with the
ferryman, till I had searched for my slippers. I went
upstairs, carrying with me a little knife, which had an
exceeding sharp edge, and with it I cut four beds, till I
had done damage to the value of upwards of fifty
crowns. I then returned to the ferry, with some scraps of
bed-clothes in my pocket, and ordered the person who
held the cable to which the ferry was tied to set off with
all speed.

And this was the act of a distinguished artist
of acknowledged reputation, and a man of thirty-
five!

Alessandro de' Medici now reigned in Florence.
He received Cellini with great kindness and employed him at once to design a new coinage. But
he quarrelled with another of the Medicis, and,
having received full pardon from the Pope, settled
again in Rome. Things did not go well with him.
He complained that the Pope did not pay him
properly for a golden cover that he had made for

an illuminated horn book that was presented to the Emperor Charles V, and he had other reasons for believing that he was out of favour. He therefore left the city secretly, and went first to Venice and then to Paris, hoping to receive employment from the King of France. But he fell ill with a fever and returned to Rome, where, on information supplied by a workman with whom he had quarrelled, he was accused of stealing some of the jewels entrusted to him by Clement VII. He was arrested and imprisoned in the Castle of St. Angelo, which he had, as he has related, so heroically defended. The governor of the prison was mad, and Cellini relates with gusto incredible stories of his eccentricities. Even more highly coloured is the story of his escape from prison. The late J. A. Symonds has declared that Cellini was a good Catholic, apparently believing that a good Catholic can be a great rogue, and it is certainly true that on occasion he was glib with religious phrases. He begins the story of his escape from the castle as follows: "I began with praying fervently to Almighty God that it would please His

Divine Majesty to befriend and assist me in that hazardous enterprise." Then he proceeded with a pair of pincers, which he had stolen from one of the guards, to take the hinges off the door of his cell and to cut his sheet into long strips. He climbed over three walls, at the third falling, breaking a leg and bruising his head, and he lay on the ground half insensible for an hour and a half:

I then crept on my hands and knees towards the gate, with my dagger in my hand, and, upon coming up to it, found it shut; but observing a stone under the gate, and thinking that it did not stick very fast, I prepared to push it away; clapping my hands to it, I found that I could move it with ease, so I soon pulled it out, and effected my egress. It was about five hundred paces from the place where I had had my fall to the gate at which I entered the city.

As soon as I got in, some mastiff dogs came up, and bit me severely: finding that they persisted to worry me I took my dagger and gave one of them so severe a stab, that he set up a loud howling; whereupon all the dogs in the neighbourhood, as is the nature of those animals, ran up to him; and I made all the haste I could to crawl towards the church of St. Maria Transpontina.

He bribed a water carrier to take him to the steps of St. Peter's on his donkey and from there he started to crawl again, and he finally found refuge at the house of Cardinal Cornaro. But his friends were not able to save him, and he was soon back again at St. Angelo, this time being locked in a very dark room under the garden where there was "a great quantity of water full of tarantulas and other poisonous insects." Again, according to his own story, Cellini endured the miseries of his confinement with exemplary patience. He was given a Bible "in the vulgar tongue" —it may be startling to good English Protestants to learn that Italians could read the Bible in Italian when Tyndall had hardly finished his English version—and he says: "I commenced the Bible from the beginning and perused it every day with so much attention and took so much delight in it that if it had been in my power I should have done nothing else but read." Despite his sufferings he says that he often sang and prayed and "sometimes wrote with a compound of brickdust."

After some time he was put into a more comfortable cell, and was finally released through the good offices of the Cardinal of Ferrara, the brother-in-law of Lucrezia Borgia, who came from Francis I of France to beg that he might engage his services. The Pope was anxious to please the French King and signed the order of release. The artist had once more saved the criminal. Paul, indeed, was very glad to get Cellini out of Rome. Such was the culture of the times that it would have been a far more unpopular act to hang an artist than to burn a saint, and Cellini was much too troublesome and too truculent to be permitted again to live a free man in the Eternal City. Indeed, Cellini was no sooner out of prison than he had qualified to return. On Good Friday, while journeying from Rome to Ferrara, where he stayed with the Cardinal before setting out for France, he started to quarrel with the postmaster, who accused him of having ridden his horses too hard, and the quarrel soon became a scuffle. The postmaster threatened Cellini with his pike:

When I saw him thus determined, I, to keep him off for a while, presented the muzzle of my piece at him. He, notwithstanding, flew at me with redoubled fury; and the gun which I held in my hand, though in a proper position for my own defence, was not rightly levelled at him, but, the muzzle being raised aloft, it went off of itself. The ball hit against the arch over the street door, and having rebounded, entered the postmaster's wind-pipe, who instantly fell dead upon the ground.

Francis of France was at Fontainbleau when Cellini joined his Court, and presented to him a cup and basin that he had made. Expressing his thanks, the King said: "It is my real opinion that the ancients were never capable of working in so exquisite a taste. I have seen all the masterpieces of the greatest artists of Italy, but never before beheld anything that gave me such high satisfaction."

This was a good beginning, but strong disagreement soon arose concerning the yearly sum to be paid to the artist. He was offered three hundred crowns, and in high disgust he mounted his horse and declared that he would ride back to Italy. Then he was offered seven hundred crowns with additional payments for all work that he did and five hundred crowns to cover the cost of his journey to France. He was given Le Petit Nesle in Paris, on the left bank of the Seine, as a house and work-shop, and he proceeded with his tireless energy to perhaps the greatest work of his life. Among other beautiful things that he made was the often photographed salt-cellar that is now in Vienna. But, wherever he went, Cellini always succeeded in making enemies, and in France he was unlucky enough to make a very dangerous enemy in the person of the King's mistress, Madame d'Étampes. To secure her goodwill he had called on her to present her with an exquisite little vase. With the arrogance of her kind, she kept him waiting in her ante-room for hours, and Cellini, who could never endure slights, left in a rage and gave the vase to a cardinal. Madame d'Étampes was furious. "The rage of this vindictive woman," says Cellini, "kept continually on the increase," while the lady declared: "It is I who rule the world, yet a little fellow like Benvenuto Cellini has the impudence to snap his fingers at me." Rivals were encouraged. The Italian was constantly abused to the King. His position grew more and more difficult and—

this always annoyed Cellini most—money due to him was often not forthcoming.

In 1545 Cellini returned from France to Florence, to be warmly received by his family, to whom he was always strikingly generous. The young astute and scrupulous Cosimo de' Medici now ruled the city, insisting that the citizens should respect the decencies of life, in a manner that recalled Savonarola. Cosimo welcomed Cellini to his native city, and gave him the order for the famous statue of Perseus. The story of the trials that awaited the artist before Perseus was finished has often been told. He was ill. He was overworked. He was worried by accusations from France. His inherent viciousness caused a very foul charge to be made against him, probably not without reason. Cosimo was difficult, and patron and artist often quarrelled. At the last moment, when everything was ready for the casting, Cellini had a bad attack of fever and his workmen neglected their tasks. But all difficulties were overcome and Perseus emerged triumphant. "I have known you for many years as the greatest goldsmith of whom we have any information," wrote Michael Angelo, "and henceforward I shall know you for a sculptor of like quality." Cellini went to Rome to see his friend and to offer his services to the new Pope, Julius III, but he was soon acute enough to realise that there never again would be a welcome for him at the papal court. In his *Memoirs* there are constant references to the ill-conduct of ecclesiastics, but he can hardly be taken as an impartial witness.

Madame d'Étampes had made trouble for Cellini in Paris, and the Grand Duchess, a Spanish lady of many virtues but of uncomfortable pride, made trouble for him at Florence. He was tactless, as he always was with women, and she encouraged her husband to the niggardliness which always drove Cellini to furious indiscretion. He was asked at what sum he valued his Perseus. He replied that artists could not put prices on their work, but he added that ten thousand crowns would not be too much. The Duke laughed. With ten thousand crowns, he said, cities and great palaces are built. "Your Excellency," Cellini replied, "can find multitudes of men who can build cities and palaces, but cannot find one man in the whole world who can make another Perseus." He finally agreed to accept three thousand five hundred crowns, part of which was never paid. Cellini was in serious trouble twice again before the end of his life and was imprisoned on charges of what J. A. Symonds has called "criminal immorality." In 1564, when he was sixty-four, he married and had two children, a son and a daughter, but there is no record of any work of importance done in his later years. He was old and weary and perhaps out of fashion. He died in 1571.

As the author of *Chisel, Pen, and Poignard* has said, "he was a sculptor, an author, a goldsmith, a gunsmith, an engineer, an enameller, an artillery-man, a swordsman, a sportsman, a bronze caster, a poet-taster, and a performer on the cornet à piston." It might be added that he was also a murderer, a thief, a forger, and a man of blatant and disgusting immorality. His *Memoirs* are most admirable reading, but they are perhaps the most unmoral book ever written. Rousseau's *Confessions* are unctuous. Cellini's confessions are unconscious.

He describes his vices as if they were the greatest virtues.

Of his wickedness there can be no question. He was a complete scoundrel. He was also a supreme craftsman, and the sixteenth century, with its keen appreciation of craftsmanship, was willing to balance one against the other. The twentieth century would be far less tolerant. A Cellini, were he born now, would go early to the gallows, or would have his heart broken and his imagination dampened down in the solitude of a whitewashed cell in a hygienic prison, and the beautiful things of which he dreamed would never be made.

THOMAS CROMWELL

THOMAS CROMWELL

1485–1540

THOMAS CROMWELL

MR. CHESTERTON contemptuously dismisses Thomas Cromwell as "a dirty fellow." To Froude he is one of the great figures of the Reformation. As has been well said, Cromwell as a Protestant martyr is very much like Frederick the Great as a Protestant hero, but, such is the perversity of hero-worship, Cromwell is a hero to Froude, and the unspeakable Frederick to Carlyle.

Cromwell played a part of the very first importance in English history. For ten years he held high office. For six years he was a virtual dictator, and in those six years he destroyed what could never be reconstructed, and incidentally made the fortune of the class that was successfully to revolt against the King in the next century and virtually to rule England for two and a half centuries. Cromwell himself was inhuman, a monster impossible to understand. It is quite human to do evil that evil may come. It is possibly defensible to do evil that good may come. But it is appalling to do evil that nothing may come. Some men have plotted and lied and betrayed to gain position; others to gain wealth. Cromwell does not seem to have had any particular overmastering personal ambition. He had a comfortable middle-class income before he entered official life. His service with Wolsey must have taught him the uncertain temper of the King and the probability that a swift fall was the certain sequel to high favour. He must have anticipated his fate, and he certainly did nothing during his official life to propitiate hostility or to make friends.

His one ambition was to test the political theory which he had apparently learned from Machiavelli. He had the same kind of mind as the ruthless modern biologist who, having evolved a certain theory, quite probably of the very smallest importance, proceeds to test its reliability by inflicting the most painful of deaths on a couple of hundred rabbits. Cromwell established in England what Green calls the New Monarchy, the character of which would be more correctly implied by the phrase the New Tyranny. He came back from Italy convinced that personal rule was the only effective rule, and he knew that, while an established dictatorship may perhaps be tolerant and benevolent—I confess that there is little evidence to prove that this surmise is true—dictatorships can only be established by the ruthless suppression of opposition and criticism. This was afterwards discovered perhaps somewhat to his own surprise, by Robespierre. It was thoroughly realised by Lenin when he launched the Bolshevist revolution, and it has been quite properly and reasonably accepted by Mussolini. It may be taken as a political axiom that to create a dictatorship you must first create a Terror, and the Terror established by Cromwell in the England of the sixteenth century was much more thorough, much more efficient, and much more horrible, than the amateur effort of the French Revolutionists.

The contention that the Reformation in England was, as Froude pretends, the revolt of a great-hearted, freedom-loving people against a foreign tyrant is the sheerest nonsense. The adherence of the Government of Great Britain to the cause of the Reformation was one consequence of the attempt of that Government to establish itself as an autocracy, and it was not so much the international power of the Pope that had to be repudiated as the enormous influence of the Church in the realm of England that had to be destroyed. Whether that power was beneficent or maleficent was beside the point. Whether it was approved or repudiated by the people was a matter of entire indifference to Thomas Cromwell. The power of the Church was a rival to the power of the King. So long as the Church was permitted to remain wealthy and influential, the authority of the throne was always open to challenge. The great nobles had been broken. Parliament was subservient. The people were inarticulate. But the Church, with its international mandate and its indefinite spiritual charter, blocked the way to autocracy. That is the reason, and the only reason, why Thomas Cromwell contrived the murder of Fisher and More, why he raided the monasteries, why he prepared the way for the Elizabethan settlement. The tyranny that he sought to establish was never complete, and flickered out for ever when Charles I lost his head, but in the six years of his power, and in the pursuit of a purely secular ambition, Cromwell cut England off from the body of Western Christiandom and grafted on the constitution of the Church of England Erastian excrescences which have prejudiced her character, limited her influence, and stimulated the growth of schism and unbelief.

Thomas Cromwell was born, probably in 1485, at Putney. His father belonged to the not too successful middle class, and at one time and another was a brewer, a smith, and an armourer. Thomas ran away from home, went to Italy, and served with the murderous Condotierri, the most reckless and most efficient of mercenaries, acquiring cosmopolitan experience and the ruthlessness that characterised him as a statesman. Tiring of soldiering, he took to trading in Italy and the Low Countries, and returned to England in 1512 to marry a lady, Elizabeth Wykyes, with whose dowry he set up in business as a wool merchant, his connection with Italy and Flanders proving exceedingly useful to him. While he was still selling wool he was dabbling in law, and in 1524 he began to devote himself entirely to his legal practice. He acquired a considerable position in the City of London, and in 1523 was elected to the House of Commons. In Parliament, where he made a sensible, realistic speech on the war with France, this man of affairs was considerably bored by the waste of time which has always characterised deliberative assemblies. At the end of the session he wrote:

I have endured a Parliament which continued by the space of seventeen whole weeks, where we communed of war, peace, strife, contention, debate, murmur, grudge, riches, poverty, penury, truth, falsehood, justice, equity, deceit, oppression, magnanimity, activity, force, temperance, treason, murder, felony, and also how a commonwealth might be edified and continued within our realm. Howbeit, in conclusion we have done as our predecessors have been wont to do; that is to say, as well as we might, and left where we began.

Although he had not hesitated to attack Wolsey's policy, the great Cardinal was attracted by his ability and engaged him as one of his men of business. His first commission was the disso-

lution of the smaller monasteries, suppressed under
a Papal bull, the possessions of which supplied the
endowment of Christ Church, Oxford, and he accumulated a considerable sum in fees and briberies.
His confidential relations with the King's Minister
gave him a position of importance. In 1529 he
was on sufficiently close terms with Reginald Pole
to advise him to drop his high ideals of duty, with
the consequent dangerous opposition to the King's
wishes, and to study Machiavelli's *The Prince*. The
story is told by Pole himself, and has been discredited on the ground that *The Prince* was not actually
published until 1530, after Machiavelli's death.
But it was finished in 1513, and Cromwell may
have read it in manuscript while he was in Italy.
Certainly he had accepted its principles, and was
eager to put them into practice. Colet went to Italy
to hear Savonarola preach in Florence, to come
back eager to spend himself in the service of his
fellows. Cromwell went to Italy to learn from Machiavelli, and afterwards to practise what the Italian
had preached.

Before Wolsey's fall, Cromwell had become his

most trusted subordinate, and after the fall he behaved with loyalty and courage. Cavendish, in his
life of Wolsey, says:

There was no matter alleged against my Lord but
that he was ever ready furnished with a sufficient answer; so that at length for his honest behaviour in his
master's cause, he grew into such estimation in every
man's opinion, that he was esteemed to be the most
faithfullest servant to his master of all other, wherein
he was of all men greatly commended.

Even this demonstration of fidelity was Machiavellian. Cromwell knew quite well that, while the
King had been eager for Wolsey's fall, he was
anxious to save him from the revengeful schemes
of his enemies, and that to defend Wolsey in Parliament was a sure way of attracting the royal attention. He judged the King accurately, and, almost
immediately after Wolsey's death in 1531, he was
appointed a royal councillor, being introduced to
the sovereign by the Duke of Norfolk.

From his young manhood, Henry was impatient
of any sort of control. With no defined political
philosophy, he was determined that his will should

be the law of England, and that he should be a law unto himself. When he decided to divorce Catherine of Aragon and to marry Anne Boleyn, he was first astonished and the infuriated that any power, either in England or outside of it, should hinder the royal will. It must be admitted that in his application for annulment he had ample precedent for expecting a favourable reply. But Rome hesitated, and Wolsey's unforgivable offence was the half-hearted manner in which he supported the demand.

When Cromwell was admitted to the royal council, the King had thoroughly determined to get rid of Catherine, whatever might be the cost and whatever might be the consequences. It is often said that the suggestion that England was compelled to change her religion because Henry VIII wanted to change his wife is a frivolous misinterpretation of the facts. But the frivolous is often the true, and it can hardly be denied that, but for Anne Boleyn, Henry would neither have quarrelled with the Pope nor have become the ally of Protestant princes, with whose religion he had never the smallest sympathy. The situation was exactly suited for the developments that Cromwell desired. The hot-blooded, angry monarch was ready to use any means to attain his end, and the wily Italianised scrivener whispered in his ear that the obvious way was to repudiate the papal authority, and by the exercise of his own supremacy in Church and State to compel the English ecclesiastical authorities to declare his first marriage invalid. Cromwell saw in Henry his English Cesare Borgia, whom he could cajole into the experiment in tyranny on which he had set his heart, and it was obvious policy to per-suade the King to embark on autocracy as a means of gaining the woman whom his heart desired. Henry listened and hesitated. He still regarded him-self as a faithful son of the Catholic Church. He was timorous of risking the wrath of Rome, and was still hopeful that the Pope might be persuaded to grant him the favour that he sought. Though he hesitated, he listened eagerly, and in the two years that passed before the marriage with Catherine was dissolved, on the authority of Cranmer, and Anne Boleyn became Queen of England, the influence of

Cromwell became predominant in the royal councils.

Reginald Pole, who, with his many fine qualities, was addicted to exaggeration and hysteria, has left a fantastic account of Cromwell's first ominous interview with the King. He puts a long speech into Cromwell's mouth in which he tries to persuade Henry that a king may always do as he pleases, without regard to the laws of God or man, adding that Henry would be perfectly justified in denying the authority of the Pope and proclaiming himself head of the Church in England. Pole had probably acted on Cromwell's suggestion and had read *The Prince*, and there is nothing improbable in the speech with which he credits the "Devil's Nuncio," though at the best it is only fiction founded on fact.

Cromwell was the possessor of a considerable fortune, amounting to some sixty thousand pounds in modern money, when he became the royal Minister. His rascalities, therefore, cannot be excused on the ground that even rogues must live. In 1534 he was all powerful, and from that date to his fall he was, in effect, the master of England. He had packed the Parliament, and the King had become his creature. He had given him the woman whom he desired, and subsequently he gave him the wealth that he coveted.

Cromwell's first business as a Minister was to enforce general obedience to the law and to suppress the prevalent crime and brigandage, and in this he was successful by means of a not excessive severity. But administrative reform was a secondary consideration. Almost from his entrance into the royal council he began a well-considered struggle with the Church. Convocation was compelled to acknowledge the King as "the only supreme head of the Church," though Fisher insisted on the qualifying clause, "so far as the law of Christ permits." The clergy were condemned to a fine of nearly a million pounds in modern money for breaking the Statute of Præmunire in admitting Wolsey's claim to legatine authority. In 1532 Parliament passed the Annates Act, which relieved English bishops from sending to Rome the whole of their first year's revenue. Many of the bishops, understanding the royal intention, were opposed to this Act, but it was to be suspended during the King's pleasure, and the intention was a threat to Rome of a considerable loss in income derived from England unless the Pope would agree to the divorce. In 1532 a move was made against the judges of the Church courts, and it was clear that the campaign of Henry II against the Church was to be imitated in much more favourable circumstances. The aged Archbishop Warham, the friend of Erasmus and the patron of the new learning, died in this year, weary of the perplexities of the times, and the pliant Cranmer was appointed to Canterbury in his place.

The divorce was the breaking-point with Western Christendom. Cromwell knew that it must be. Henry hoped that he might be permitted to live in a sort of semi-allegiance to Rome. But, two months after Cranmer had delivered his judgment, Clement made the position perfectly clear by a formal declaration in which he pronounced the marriage to Anne a mockery and her children illegitimate, adding the threat that he would excommunicate Henry unless he took Catherine back. This was

[103]

exactly what Cromwell had hoped for. A King threatened must at once hit back, and Henry hit back with the Act of Succession, legitimatising Anne's children, and the Act of Supremacy, definitely repudiating the Pope's authority. An oath of obedience to the Act of Supremacy was demanded from clergy and laity, and was generally subscribed. The most famous recalcitrants were Fisher, the aged Bishop of Rochester, best loved of English prelates, and Thomas More, the ex-Chancellor, most lovable of English statesmen. With them were a number of Franciscan friars, who were expelled from their houses, driven into exile, thrown into prison, left to die of hunger. Fisher and More were committed to the Tower in 1534. While they were awaiting their fate, the friars of three Carthusian houses were condemned to death as traitors for refusing to subscribe to the Act of Supremacy. This act of tyranny was passed without any open expression of public feeling, and Cromwell grew bolder. Fisher's fate was sealed by the Pope sending him a cardinal's hat while he was still in the Tower. He was executed in 1535, the last of the

English prelates who had rejoiced at the coming of the new learning. More was beheaded a few days afterwards. Cranmer, always facing both ways, urged that the executions would be a great political blunder, but they were necessary to Cromwell's policy. The Church had to be broken.

More died as he lived, a fascinating, godly man, dowered with an immense sense of humour. He was a Catholic in the very best sense of the term, and in his *Utopia* he recognised that social obligation of the faith which was to find its practical expression in the Counter-Reformation with St. Philip Neri and St. Vincent de Paul. "When did nature," wrote Erasmus, "mould a temper more gentle, endearing, and happy than the temper of Thomas More?" His execution by Cromwell was as monstrous as the execution of Danton by Robespierre, and as necessary from the same point of view. Tyranny cannot tolerate a critic, and particularly a critic with a sense of humour. Perhaps there is no example in literature of more absurd fanaticism than Froude's apology for the killing of a man for whom he himself expresses admiration.

"It was, at once," he says, "most piteous and most inevitable. The hour of retribution had come at length, when at the hands of the Roman Church was to be required all the righteous blood which it had shed, from the blood of Raymond of Toulouse to the blood of the last victim who had blackened into ashes at Smithfield. The voices crying underneath the altar had been heard upon the throne of the Most High, and woe to the generation of which the dark account had been demanded." Raymond of Toulouse, by the way, was not put to death, but was reconciled to the Church, and it was the voice of Machiavelli to which Thomas Cromwell listened and certainly not the voices from underneath the altar.

The next step in the institution of the tyranny was the Treasons Act, which finally established the Terror in England. Mr. Chesterton calls it "a government by torturers rendered ubiquitous by spies." Froude himself admits that "Cromwell, whose especial gift it was to wind himself into the secrets of the clergy, had his sleuth hounds abroad whose scent was not easily baffled." The country was infested by an army of sneaking informers. It was dangerous to whisper criticism. No man was safe, and the unscrupulous could remove rivals in commerce or in love by repeating to the spies some hasty, inconsidered word. A cloud of fear settled over England. "Men felt," Erasmus wrote, "as if a scorpion lay sleeping under every stone." Torture was used to compel the innocent to reveal their thoughts, and to force priests to repeat the secrets of the confessional. It was unsafe to speak even behind closed doors. "Friends who used to write and send me presents," Erasmus says, "now send neither letter nor gifts nor receive any from anywhere, and this through fear."

It was against the clergy that the Treasons Act was mainly used, and the "evidence" quoted at great length by Froude, and used for the undoing of the accused, would be grotesque if it were not so infernally wicked. And Cromwell carried on his campaign with cold, business-like exactitude. Among his papers are to be found such records as, "*Item*. The Abbot of Reading to be sent down and executed at Reading." Everything was cut and dried. In 1536, Cromwell proceeded to earn the title of the "hammer of the monks" by the systematic spoliation of the monasteries. There were at the time seven hundred monastic establishments in England, and twenty-seven abbots had seats in Parliament. The monasteries were great landowners. The monks, on the whole, were, as Cobbett insisted, good landlords, and Mr. Chesterton has added that they at least were not absentee landlords. Besides the land, the monasteries owned libraries, beautiful and costly altar vessels, and often priceless vestments. They were rich; they were influential; they still remained to a large extent the bulwarks of the poor. They stood in the way of the King's supremacy, and, moreover, the robbery of their possessions would enable Cromwell to carry out his promise to make Henry "the richest king that had ever been in England." It is never very difficult to find a good excuse for an evil deed. Abuses unquestionably had entered into the monastic life. Worldliness had come with wealth, and sometimes austerity had given place to slackness. Rabelais had laughed his deep guffaw at the narrow minds in narrow cells. Erasmus and the humanists had demanded the reforms which were to come, alas! belatedly with St. Ignatius and St. Dominic. But the charge that at least two-thirds of the monasteries in England cried to high heaven for suppression is a gross exaggeration. The monks had retained sufficient virtue to retain the trust and affection of the common people, and so deeply did the people resent the dissolution that it almost cost Henry his throne.

The reports of the visitations made by Cromwell's creatures have no sort of value. They were sent, not to make impartial investigations, but to provide excuses for bare-faced robbery. That was the intention, and that was the achievement. The great wealth of the monasteries was not used for the furtherance of the cause of religion or of education. It was used to buy off opposition and to placate friendship, and the money stolen from the monasteries was the beginning of the fortunes of the great families that contrived the revolution of the seventeenth century and gained a long ascendancy with the accession of William III.

Cromwell proceeded warily. The poorer monasteries were suppressed first, with the consequence of a rising in Lincolnshire, and shortly afterwards the much more important revolt known as the Pilgrimage of Grace in Yorkshire. Both were suppressed with some difficulty, partly by the employment of foreign troops, partly by lying promises. The leaders, most of them inept, were gentlefolk. The rank and file were farmers and peasants, who needed no conscription. Having defeated popular rebellion, Cromwell proceeded to terrorise his highly born enemies. Reginald Pole was on the Continent, and not to be lured to England, and Cromwell endeavoured to hire an Italian bravo to assassinate him. He was dangerous. His indictment of Henry's policy was effective, despite its exaggerations. Henry was formally excommunicated in 1538, and it was suspected that Pole had urged the Pope to this last step, and the mean revenge was the arrest and execution of his aged mother, Margaret Plantagenet, Countess of Salisbury, a princess of the royal blood.

Rumours of a rising in the west, probably due

to the activity of *agents provocateurs,* was the excuse for further monastic suppressions. On November 15th, 1539, the Abbot of Glastonbury was executed on the ridiculous charge of robbing his own monastery. The Abbot of Reading was hanged on the same day. The Abbot of Colchester was hanged a fortnight later, and by the end of the year the "standing army of the Pope" was broken. One million pounds in modern money was the value of the portable property that was stolen. The value of the sequestrated lands was nearly ten million pounds, and miscellaneous profits amounted to nearly another million. Truly a highly profitable achievement! Cromwell had his share of the loot. From his own accounts it appears that in the last three years of his life he acquired property to the value of nearly half a million pounds sterling. He built himself a large mansion in the City of London, which he furnished in imitation of the great houses that he had seen years before in Italy. He gave great parties. He kept a hundred horses, and two hundred poor men were fed twice a day at his gate, and in April 1540 he entered the House of Lords as the Earl of Essex.

But Cromwell had shot his bolt. For six years Henry—a very portly Borgia, without Cesare's complete unscrupulousness—had played the part for which his Minister had cast him. But Cromwell, who, himself, had no religion, did not realise that Henry still most firmly believed all the assertions of the Catholic creed, and that, for all his obstinacy, he was seriously frightened by the excommunication. He was, moreover, disgusted by the extravagances of the extreme Protestants whom Cromwell patronised because their support was necessary for him, and the King certainly warmly sympathised with the ten thousand citizens of London who forcibly resented the prosecution of a Catholic preacher. The bear was growing weary of being led, and was longing for an excuse for ridding himself of his bear-leader, and the excuse was forthcoming.

In the summer of 1540, Henry was looking for a fourth wife. The one son that Jane Seymour had borne him was sickly and unlikely to live, and he was fearful for the continuance of his dynasty. Suggestions were made to various royal ladies, but were politely declined. "If I had two heads," said one of them, "I might marry the King of England." The break with Rome had seemed necessary to Cromwell in order that the autocracy might be established. The rupture had antagonised both the Emperor and the King of France, who declined Cromwell's suggestion that he should enter into a league with England and the German Lutheran princes against Spain and the Empire. Cromwell was, therefore, forced to negotiate an entirely Protestant alliance against the Catholic powers, the alliance which Elizabeth resisted during the greater part of her reign and to which she was finally compelled. As a preliminary to this international arrangement, he arranged the marriage of Henry with Anne of Cleves. Poor Anne was a good and kindly princess, but she was very fat and ugly. When Henry met her at Rochester he came away "looking very sad and pensive," afterwards lamenting the fate of princes "to be in matters of marriage of far worse sort than the condition of poor men," and from the day of his marriage he was "in a manner weary of his life." And the marriage was a political failure. The German Protestant princes thought it far more advisable to make friends with the Emperor Charles, who was at their door, rather than to bother about the English King, who was many miles away. Henry had gained nothing with his unattractive wife, and he promptly demanded another divorce. But this for Cromwell would have been fatal. It would have outraged the Protestants as the Catholics had been outraged by the divorce from Catherine, and he declared it impossible. As he had risen by providing the King with the wife that he wanted, so he fell by providing the King with a wife that he did not want. And he was surrounded with enemies eager for his fall.

He was arrested in the Privy Council Chamber and taken to the Tower. The Parliamentary Bill of Attainder was elaborate. In most of the offences of which Cromwell was accused, the King had been an eager accomplice. Among other things, he was charged with being a detestable heretic. Cranmer alone dared to defend him, but his intervention was useless. Henry was weary of his Minister, and Cromwell had taught him that a wise prince removes servants who are no longer of use. He was beheaded on July 28th, 1540. Many, it is related, lamented, but more rejoiced.

Unemotional, uninfluenced by the motives that affect the majority of men, Cromwell carried through his experiment and was probably not in the least surprised at the price he had to pay. He was the chief agent of the English Reformation, not in the least because he desired the reformation of the Church, but because Machiavellian rule in England was impossible without breaking the power of the Church. He was a reckless experimenter, and dearly have generations of Englishmen paid for his skill and his persistence.

MAZARIN

JULES MAZARIN
1602–1661

MAZARIN

THROUGH the ages Italy has suffered grievous things from the lust of conquest of French princes, and, perhaps as compensation, three Italian adventurers have held France in thrall—the Sicilian Mazarin, the Corsican Napoleon Bonaparte, and the Genoese Gambetta. Like Louis XI, Mazarin is the victim of a great romantic writer. As the world knows Louis XI from Scott, so it knows Mazarin from Dumas. The crafty Sicilian adventurer is the arch-villain of the drama in which d'Artagnan, Athos, Porthos, and Aramis are the gorgeous heroes, trembling and foiled by the valour and resource of his opponents. Dumas described Mazarin as "that mean fellow who tries to put on his head a crown which he has stolen under a pillow; that puppy who calls his party that of the king and who bethought himself of putting the princes of the blood into prison, not daring to kill them as did the great cardinal; a skinflint who weighs his golden crowns and keeps the clipped ones from fear that although he cheats he may lose them at his next day's game." That is the Mazarin of fiction. The Mazarin of fact was a different figure, unscrupulous, unattractive, but with at least some of the qualities of greatness.

Jules Mazarin was born in 1602. His father was in the service of the Colonnas, and his mother was a kinswoman of that great family. He was educated at Rome by the Jesuits, and left them with the reputation of a model student. From his seventeenth to his twenty-second year he was at the University of Alcala, in Spain, where he learned to speak Spanish fluently and acquired the intimate knowledge of the Spanish character which was to be of incalculable value to him in his dealings with the Spanish-born French Queen. On his return to Rome, he was entrusted by the Pope, Urban VIII, with a diplomatic mission, which he fulfilled with great success, and his reward included canonries at St. John Lateran and Santa Maria Maggiore, although he was only in minor orders. Mazarin was never ordained priest, and probably never even ordained deacon.

His gifts for negotiation were proved again in 1629, when the French and Spanish troops were manœuvring before the beginning of hostilities. Mazarin, the papal agent, galloped between the two armies with the recently signed treaty in his hands, loudly shouting, "Peace, peace." It was a theatrical entrance on to the great stage of European affairs. In 1634, he was appointed Papal Nuncio at Paris. Richelieu recognised his great qualities, and, though he was an Italian and the diplomatic representative of the Vatican, the Cardinal offered him employment in the service of the French King. Although the Reformation and the disruption of Europe had occurred a hundred years before, there was still a remnant left of the old European spirit, and there was nothing in the least shameful, and, indeed, nothing unusual, in a talented Italian taking service with France. Indeed, in the civil commotions that occurred during the years of Mazarin's domination, French princes like Condé and Turenne had no compunction and no sense of treason in allying themselves with the Spaniards against the French Crown. The narrow faith of nationalism, that has been for generations the most powerful influence in Europeon affairs, had still to be fully developed.

Mazarin gladly accepted Richelieu's offer. He was eager for a wider outlet for his abilities than the papal service afforded, and he realised that the Cardinal's hat, then more commonly the reward of statesmanship than of piety, would never be his unless he had the backing of a powerful foreign prince. It was in 1639 that he became a naturalised Frenchman.

In introducing Mazarin to Queen Anne, Richelieu said, "You will like him, madame; he resembles Buckingham." Anne of Austria is the peerless heroine of Dumas, and the story of Buckingham and the diamond studs is the incident round which the magician has woven the adventures of the Musketeers. It is certain that Buckingham, perhaps the most reckless incompetent ever entrusted with a delicate foreign mission, fell in love with the French Queen. It is probable that Anne was not insensible to his superficial charm, and that she may have been indiscreet, as she afterwards was with Montmorency, who wore a bracelet with her picture on his arm. But it is doubtful whether Anne was ever more than indiscreet, and it cannot be forgotten that it suited Richelieu to exaggerate her indiscretions. The relations between her and her husband, Louis XIII, were always strained. Louis strongly resembled his unfortunate successor Louis XVI. Inherited ill health had been emphasised by the violent treatment of physicians, who in one year bled him seven times, made him swallow two hundred and twelve purgatives, and gave him two hundred and fifteen injections. He was pious, secretive, conscientious, and not unintelligent, and his subjection to Richelieu was not so much evidence of feebleness of purpose as of realisation of his Minister's supreme gifts. From the beginning, the policy of the great Cardinal was anti-Spanish. Anne was a Spaniard, with little idea of international politics and no conception of patriotism as it is understood to-day. The Cardinal was the enemy of her family and her friends, and was therefore her enemy. In so far as it was possible, she opposed his plans, with the consequence of creating for herself an enemy whose cold determination made twenty years of her life bitter and fearful.

After the birth of her son, the future Louis XIV, in 1638, and until her husband's death, Anne ceased altogether to concern herself with intrigue, and her doors were no longer thrown wide open to that supreme mistress of political plotting, the beautiful Madame de Chevreuse. She had ceased to be a Spanish princess. She was the mother of a king of France. Anne was a handsome woman, healthy and plump, with fine eyes and fair hair. She was indolent, rarely awakening in the morning till eleven, and her appetite was immense. Both in her dress and in her manner she was strikingly modest. Unlike her mother-in-law, the fat widow of Henry IV, Marie de Medici, she spoke French without the trace of an accent, and when it was possible she escaped from the oppressive etiquette of her Court—by no means so oppressive, by the way, as it was to be during the reign of her son— and was pleasantly unconventional. She was very devout, simple, and coquettish, as many good women are, and no great lady ever knew so well how to grow old gracefully. In the early days of her son's great reign she was to be a figure of charm and dignity, and he always had for her a deep affection and unfailing respect.

Two years after Mazarin settled in Paris, he secured the coveted Cardinal's hat, and Richelieu died. Richelieu nominated the Italian as his successor, and immediately after his death the King gave orders that all matters of State were to be referred to the Sicilian. Louis died two years afterwards. On the death of her husband, the Queen acted promptly and with great discretion, almost certainly following Mazarin's counsel. It is doubtful when the close friendship between Queen and Minister actually began. The story that they were married may or may not be true, but that they were lovers is an established historical fact.

In his will the King had endeavoured materially to limit the powers of his widow as regent for his four-years'-old son, and Anne appealed to the Parliament of Paris to set aside its provisions. Anne met the Parliament with the baby King, who was seated on the Bed of Justice and had been coached with a speech, of which he declined to say a word. Her charm and determination, however, conquered, and she obtained a free hand, which she at once used, much to the surprise of the greedy and expectant, by confirming Mazarin in his office. Never did courtier know so well how to treat a sovereign lady, independent for the first time in her life, jealous of her authority, and yet more than a little afraid of herself. He was always suave, always eager to explain, always respectful, always apparently caring much more for his mistress than for himself. As time went on and confidence became greater, the Cardinal grew more assertive and the mistress more pliant, and less than eighteen months after the death of Louis XIII, the Queen informed the council that she had granted Mazarin apartments in the Palais Royal, where the royal family lived, "so as to be able to confer with him on her business more conveniently."

At the beginning, Anne was immensely popular with the people, and Mazarin shared her popularity. The Cardinal de Retz says in the Memoirs, from which most of our knowledge of the period is derived: "On the steps of the throne, whence the terrible Richelieu had crushed rather than ruled the human race, we saw a successor who was gentle, benign, who desired nothing for himself but was in despair because his dignity as Cardinal did not permit him to humiliate himself before all the world as he fain would have done." "The great strength of M. the Cardinal de Mazarin," says another contemporary, "lay in soft words, hinting, giving reason to hope." And Fr. Tixier confessed: "I have never approached the Cardinal without being persuaded I was going to talk to the greatest impostor in the world, and I never left his presence without being charmed by him."

It was not to be expected that things would go smoothly for long, or that seventeenth-century Paris would cease from its characteristic plottings, particularly with a child on the throne and an inexperienced woman as regent. But Mazarin knew, and Mazarin struck boldly. One morning Paris learned that the Duc de Beaufort, grandson of

Henri IV, was in the castle of Vincennes, and that Madame de Chevreuse had been banished to Toulouse. "The morning after the events," wrote de Retz, "the Cardinal seemed more moderate and civil than ever. Access to his person was quite free. Audiences were easily granted. People dined with him just as with any private individual. He even put away a great deal of the stately manner affected by cardinals of the most ordinary sort. In effect, he played his cards so well that he had his foot on everybody's head while everybody thought he was still standing beside them."

The strong hand with high-born plotters was used at the most auspicious moment. Anne's regency began with a great military victory. The long nightmare of the Thirty Years' War was drawing to an end when Richelieu and Louis died. It had been the policy of the great Cardinal to break the power of the Empire and to destroy the Spanish domination of Europe, but the great plan was not attained until after his death. In 1643, the Duc d'Enghien, eldest son of the Prince de Condé, a young man of twenty-two, slovenly in his dress, unattractive in appearance, and ungainly in carriage, was placed in command of a French army sent to oppose a Spanish invasion of Champagne from the Low Countries. Richelieu had bound the Condés to him by marrying the Duc d'Enghien, much against his will, to one of his nieces. Mazarin appointed him to this high command that he might secure the reversion of the Condé influence. Acting according to his own genius, and disregarding the warnings of experienced commanders, d'Enghien won the great victory of Rocroi, which was the first step in establishing French military superiority in Europe and the beginning of the military glory of the reign of Louis XIV. Rocroi was followed by a series of successful campaigns conducted by d'Enghien and Turenne, one of the greatest of all French generals. The fortune of war ebbed and flowed, and there were occasional set-backs for the French commanders, but both in Germany and in Flanders victory followed victory, and the Treaty of Westphalia, signed on October 24th, 1648, marks the fall of the Empire, the decadence of Spain, and the rise of France, which, among other

things, secured the frontier on the Rhine which
has always been the dream of French nationalist
statesmanship. The Regency owed a heavy debt to
the Condés. D'Enghien had won glory and profit
for France in the field of battle, and his father, the
Prince de Condé, had given Anne his steady support in Paris. The Prince was a queer creature. He
was very ugly and very dirty, and his red eyes,
matted hair, and greasy beard were a sufficient explanation of the vagaries of a beautiful wife. But
he was a shrewd politician and an excellent man
of business, and he left his son the richest of all
the subjects of France. Anne could not make friends
without making enemies. On the death of the old
Prince, his successor and his brother, the Prince
de Conti, were loaded with favours, with the consequence of arousing bitter jealousies in the hearts
of their rivals, the most influential of whom was
Gaston, Duc d'Orléans, the young King's uncle.

In order to understand the intrigues that now
gathered round Mazarin and the Queen it is necessary to know something of the curious Paris society
at the beginning of the reign of Louis XIV. Riche-

lieu had largely broken the political power of the princes and nobles. The absolute authority of the throne had been established, and, as a consequence of the political impotence of the nobles, there had grown up in Paris an aristocratic society in which intellect was regarded as of almost equal account as birth. In the salons of Madame de Rambouillet the talk was of poetry rather than of battles, and the writer was regarded with greater admiration than the soldier. It was an age of sentimental posing. The salons imitated the Courts of the Troubadours. Feminine influence was predominant. There was much talk of heroic deeds, with a horror of anything like danger—in de Retz's scornful phrase, "violence in the drawing-room and trumpets in the square." It was in these salons that Mazarin found his most sarcastic critics. But more serious danger came from a more serious cause.

Wars, even when they are successful, have to be paid for, and victories in the field mean overtaxation in the slums. In the Paris byways they cared nothing for the glory of Rocroi, but they cared a great deal for high prices and high taxation, and they ascribed all their misfortunes to the fact that France was ruled by an Italian. In 1645 the women of Paris, who have always played their part in popular risings, threw themselves at Anne's feet when she was entering Notre-Dame and cried that she "had a man about her who took everything." The Paris Parliament made itself the mouthpiece of popular discontent, and mouthed fine sentiments with many classical allusions. The Parliament was a curious semi-judicial body, the functions of which it is difficult for a foreigner to understand, with—I quote M. Boulenger—"its huge following of attorneys, sheriffs, officers, serjeants, lawyers and pettifoggers of every kind." In the seventeenth century it was consistently unpractical, unaware, and uninstructed in the course of public affairs. The salons, the over-taxed people, the ambitious Parliament, were all eager for the Cardinal's downfall. To the salons the whole thing was a comedy. The proceedings of Parliament were farcical. But there was tragedy in the streets. The three movements became formidable when they were brought together by the genius of a remarkable man, Paul de Gondi, Coadjutor to the Archbishop of Paris, whose subtle schemings have been so vividly described by Alexandre Dumas. In all the proceedings of the serio-comic attempts at revolution of the Fronde, it was Gondi who was the directing hand.

In 1648 the Queen ordered the arrest of two Paris councillors who had been loudest in their denunciation of the Cardinal and the Court. Rioting followed the arrest, and the Cardinal was forced to release the councillors. A fortnight afterwards, the Queen and the young King left Paris secretly for Rueil. Mazarin tried in vain to persuade either d'Orléans, a notorious coward, or Condé, who had now discovered that he hated "that rogue of a Sicilian," forcibly to suppress the disorder, and the Queen was compelled to sign a charter demanded by the Parliament. With infinite skill Mazarin then proceeded to win Condé back.

On the eve of Twelfth Night, 1649, the Queen and her two sons were again smuggled out of Paris to Saint-Germain-en-Laye. Paris burghers armed, while Condé was encamped outside the city with a considerable army. "Thus," says M. Boulenger, "began this burlesque warfare in which the amount of gunpowder used by the warriors was far exceeded by the quantities of ink and paper consumed by the lampooners." Conspicuous among the Frondeuses were Mme. de Longueville, de Condé's sister, a would-be heroine of romance, remembered for her protestation "I do not care for innocent pleasures," and *la grande Mademoiselle*, the giant daughter of Gaston d'Orléans. The highborn ladies and gentlemen of the Fronde "with all their pretentious and somewhat heavy gallantry, their useless and Machiavellian conspiracies, their heroism and their swagger," urged the Paris burghers to war-like attacks only to be told that the citizens had no sort of intention of exposing themselves "to *sorties* in which they might very well risk their lives."

Without much trouble an agreement was patched up which brought the Court back to Paris in August. Condé, however, now regarded himself as the saviour of the throne, and Mazarin was strong enough to arrest him and his brother and his brother-in-law in January 1650, and at the end of the same year a Spanish army, led by Turenne—change of fealty was still a commonplace—which had almost advanced to the walls of Paris, was completely defeated.

Paul de Gondi, wily coadjutor, some day to be Cardinal de Retz, had still to be reckoned with. "His whole life," said a contemporary, "from one end to the other was ruled by his will. His immorality was sublime, and his greatness of soul never failed him." He was a small man, and very short-sighted. Forced into the Church, he had all the instincts of a soldier, and, indeed, duelling and women were his two preoccupations. He was ambitious to play a large part in political affairs. He had determined to be Mazarin's successor. He used the disorders of the times with masterly skill, and he almost succeeded. Perhaps the quality of the man is most evident in the fact that when he had failed, when he had realised the character of Louis XIV, and that nothing was to be hoped by a man with his political record, he put on, not only the habit, but the manner, of a Churchman, and died, if not in the odour of sanctity, with a very worthy reputation. But in 1651, De Gondi was anything but beaten, and the Cardinal, who had fancied that his enemies were in the dust, suddenly found power slipping from his hands. All his enemies were once more united against him, and Mazarin, feeling that his life was in danger, left Paris secretly and crossed the Flemish frontier. But the Fronde never could hold together. Within a few months of Mazarin's flight, d'Orléans and Condé had violently quarrelled, and, when Louis XIV attained his legal majority in September, the league fell to pieces, to flicker up into being again when Mazarin, at the head of a small army, re-entered France in December.

For a while France was threatened with real civil war. The King and Queen gathered an army commanded by Turenne, whose service had been bought at a heavy price. Orléans and Condé, who had been reconciled and were backed by Spain, had another army, Mazarin had a little army of his own, and the Parisians wisely locked the city gates and refused to let any of them enter until they were persuaded to open the gates for Condé, whose army was thus saved from absolute annihilation by Turenne. They were no sooner in the city than Orléans and Condé commenced quarrelling again. Orléans at once took to his bed and swore that he was dying, and the only satisfaction that the Parisians could find was in persistently yelling, "Death to Mazarin!" However, by way of diversion they sacked the Hôtel de Ville and murdered five members of the Municipal Council.

In August, Mazarin went back into exile, and the King was acclaimed on his re-entry to his capital, where, four months after, Mazarin joined him, in his turn to be loudly applauded by the same people who had amused themselves by calling for his death. It was no longer an Italian Cardinal that France had to deal with, but a vigorous French king who, less than two years afterwards, himself attended a meeting of the Parliament and forbade it to discuss public affairs.

The final achievement of Mazarin's political career was the arrangement of the peace treaty with Spain. Spain gained a great deal, particularly the return of fortified towns in the Low Countries, including the immortal Ypres. But France retained possessions in the north to guard her against offensive attack, the return of all that Spain had captured in the south, and a large slice of Lorraine, while the Rhenish League became a vassal of the King of France. Mazarin gained all that Richelieu had planned.

In addition—and perhaps this was the zenith of his statecraft—the marriage was arranged between Louis and the Infanta of Spain, a marriage which was to lead to wars and diplomatic complications, and finally to establish a Bourbon dynasty on the Spanish throne. In arranging this marriage, Mazarin appeared to be acting with extreme unselfishness, as the King was hotly in love with, and was eager to marry, "the skinny Maria Mancini," one of the Cardinal's nieces. Following the example of Richelieu, Mazarin had done very well for his family. His nephew was Duc de Nevers; three of his nieces were duchesses; another was married to the Prince de Conti and was therefore a princess of the royal blood; another was the wife of Eugène of Savoy; and it would have seemed well within his ambition that Maria should have been a queen. But the Cardinal did not like Maria. She had "a contradictory and passionate spirit." She had dared to oppose her masterful uncle. Moreover, Anne of Austria desired the Spanish marriage, and it was obviously in accord with political expediency, and when a man is as expert a politician as Mazarin it is easy for him to sacrifice small personal advantage in order to achieve the success of a well-thought-out plan.

Mazarin was very rich. His fortune, when he died, amounted to two hundred million francs in modern French money. He had none of the miser's joy in amassing money for money's sake, but he loved what money would buy—books, works of art, gorgeous luxury—and the Sicilian adventurer had a natural if rather vulgar joy in emphasising his great position. "The councils were held in his chamber while he was being shaved or dressed, and often he would play with his bird or his pet monkey while people were talking business with him. He never asked anyone to be seated in his presence." Like his master, Richelieu, he had a genius for discovering talented subordinates. Among them was Colbert, who was to serve Louis XIV so well and who suggested to Mazarin the amiable plan of lending his own money to the King for short periods and at exorbitant interest. Vast revenues, too, were derived from selling public positions, from bribes, and on occasion from stealing money that should have been spent on the army and the navy.

The King, almost preternaturally shrewd in his early youth, liked Mazarin and trusted him, and in the last days of the Minister's life he and the King had long talks on public affairs, Louis listening to his wily and experienced friend and particularly taking note of the counsel that he should never again have a chief Minister, but that he should rule his country himself. Following the example of Wolsey, and more successfully, the Cardinal, some days before his death, made over his whole fortune to the King. It was a *beau geste*, and it had its reward. The King refused the gift, and bade Mazarin dispose of his fortune as he would.

Mazarin died on March 9th, 1661, fortified by the rites of the Church—queer, capable, unlikeable, astute adventurer. He brought the keen intellect of an Italian realist into the turgid, romantic politics of France of the first half of the seventeenth century. So far as foreign politics were concerned, he had inherited from Richelieu a programme which he carried out and an ambition which he achieved. It was to Richelieu and to Mazarin that the possibilities of the great reign of Louis XIV were due. Richelieu sowed, Mazarin watered, and Louis gathered the increase. In nothing did Mazarin show himself more completely a realistic politician than in the alliance which he made with Oliver Cromwell, by which he won back from the Spaniards the cities of northwestern France at the price of yielding Dunkirk to the English, knowing full well that they would never be able to hold it for long. The alliance of a King with Cromwell in the seventeenth century was as daring as an alliance of a monarchy, or even of a respectable republic, with Bolshevist Russia would be to-day.

[141]

Mazarin will live among the astutest politicians and statesmen of modern Europe. But he was mean, he was a coward, and on occasion he was a cheat. It is related in the Memoirs of the Count de Grammont:

His avidity to heap up riches was not alone confined to the thousand different means, with which he was furnished by his authority, and the situation in which he was placed. His whole pursuit was gain. He was naturally fond of gaming; but he only played to enrich himself, and therefore, whenever he found an opportunity, he cheated.

Mazarin was the Cardinal who cheated at cards.

JUDGE JEFFREYS

GEORGE JEFFREYS
1648–1689

JUDGE JEFFREYS

TYRANNY has never lacked a lawyer to carry out its orders, to find precedence for its repressions, and to cover its excesses with the appearance of decency and order. The Terror had its Fouquier-Tinville. The Stuart despotism had its Judge Jeffreys. Fouquier-Tinville was a typical lawyer. He had sold his soul to a machine. He was a man of parchment, not of flesh and blood. He had not made the laws. He was not responsible for them. It was for him to carry them out, and this he did with passionless impartiality, until his own head fell into the executioner's basket. Outside the law courts, Fouquier-Tinville was a decent man, living the ordinary decent professional man's life. Jeffreys was an entirely different person. He was a man of good birth, considerable parts, and immense ambition. But he had no scruples, no dignity, and he was born without bowels, without pity or mercy. He drank prodigiously, even for the seventeenth century. He was subject to violent bursts of passion, and he had absolutely no self-control. He was the supreme bully. His greatest joy in life was to denounce, to jeer, and to hurt. And nature had eminently fitted him for the rôle that he had chosen. Jeffreys's one passion was a genuine hatred of Whigs and Dissenters, and Macaulay, who loved them both, cannot be taken as an impartial judge, but there is a historic warrant for the famous description: "Impudence and ferocity sat upon his brow. The glare of his eyes had a fascination for the unhappy victim on whom they were fixed, yet his brow and his eyes were less terrible than the savage lines of his mouth. His yell of fury, as was said by one who had often heard it, sounded like the thunder of the Judgment Day."

My gifted friend, the late H. B. Irving, endeavoured, in a delightful but perhaps not too serious study, to refute, or at least to modify, the general estimate of Jeffreys and his career. But, ingenious as is his apology, Jeffreys remains at the end, in any impartial estimate, an offensive, bloodthirsty monster.

He was the fourth son of a Welsh country gentleman, and his family had for generations been connected with the law. In after years, one of his brothers became High Sheriff of the county of Denbighshire, another was in the diplomatic service, and a third in the Church. Little is known of his boyhood except that he went successively to Shrewsbury, which Mr. Irving suggests was then a preparatory school, to St. Paul's, where he stopped two years, and to Westminster during the headmastership of the famous Busby, who had it to his credit that sixteen bishops had been birched by his "little rod," and whose distinguished pupils included Prior, Dryden, Locke, and the headstrong and unlucky Bishop Atterbury. There is generally some serious reason for moving a boy from school to school, and Jeffreys's family appear to have regarded his future with some apprehension. His father, indeed, is reported to have said: "George, I fear that thou wilt die with thy shoes and stockings on."

He went up to Trinity, Cambridge, in 1662— again for a very brief stay. In 1663 he was entered at the Inner Temple, and he remained a student there for five years. His picture in the National Portrait Gallery shows that as a young man he was attractive looking, with well formed features, and it certainly does not suggest the ruthless Jeffreys of the Bloody Assize. During his student years, however, he was notorious for the roystering and drinking which characterised his whole life, but, like many another hard-living lawyer, he had a great capacity for work.

Jeffreys was called to the Bar when he was twenty, and almost at once acquired a considerable practice, conducting his cases with such marked ability that at twenty-three the City Fathers, shrewd judges of men and particularly of lawyers, appointed him Common Serjeant. The City was not alone in its opinion of the young lawyer, who was admitted to the friendship of the high-minded Sir Matthew Hale, a judge famous for his impartiality, and the friend of Tillotson and Stillingfleet.

When he was nineteen and before he was called, Jeffreys married the penniless daughter of a clergyman, having failed in an attempt to secure the hand of the daughter of a wealthy City merchant, and his reckless eagerness to make a career may be understood, if not condoned, when it is remembered that before he was thirty he was the father of six children. Young as he was, Jeffreys thoroughly understood the character of his clients, and to impress them he invented a little comedy suggestive of Mr. Bob Sawyer's method of advertising his medical practice in Bath. He would arrange that, as he was sitting in a coffee-house with his friends, his clerk should hurriedly rush in to tell him that a client was waiting at his chambers, and Jeffreys would impatiently answer, "Let him wait. I will come presently," the company being, of course, convinced that the young lawyer, who could afford to keep a client waiting, must have a great practice.

Jeffreys was a City judge. All his interests were in the City, and the City was Whig, but for some reason, difficult to understand, he determined, if it were possible, to transfer his allegiance and services to the Court. In this he showed eminently bad judgment. The successful political adventurer must be able accurately to estimate the comparative

[149]

value of political tendencies. It is easy to be wise after the event, but acquaintance with the earlier history of the seventeenth century, and some understanding of the English character and the prejudices of the times, should have surely taught a man, concerned only for his own advancement, that the extravagances of the Restoration Court, with the humiliating subjection to France, were quickly destroying the popularity due to the reaction against Puritanism, while the possibility of a peaceful reign for the King's brother, who not only belonged to an unpopular religion, but was incompetent and narrow-minded, was extremely small. Since self-interest would appear to have dictated remaining in the City camp, it is suggested that high political principle, devotion to the Crown and to the English Church, made Jeffreys eager to leave it. But that is hard to believe. The truth is that Jeffreys was passionate and impulsive, far more than calculating.

He was probably bored by the City. He yearned for the joys of Whitehall, and he contrived to obtain an introduction to the King through Mr.

Thomas Chiffinch, in effect the royal pander, whom Evelyn describes as "His Majesty's Closet Keeper," and of whom it was said that "he had carried the abuse of backstairs influence to scientific perfection." Jeffreys was at once able to prove his usefulness by some confidential work for the Royal Council, and he became intimate with the King's favourite, the Duchess of Portsmouth, that French monument of greed. Mr. Irving quotes a lampoon describing the Duchess as:

> Monmouth's tamer, Jeff's advance,
> Foe to England, spy of France,
> False and foolish, proud and bold,
> Ugly, as you see, and old.

The Earl of Danby, who in 1673 had become head of the Administration, was one of the Duchess's lovers. As a statesman he had inherited the Clarendon tradition, and was a man of energy and some principles. But his one idea of how to govern was to bribe. He was compelled against his better judgment to be an accomplice in Charles's French plots, and he was brought down by Shaftesbury's ingenious use of Titus Oates and the Popish plots. Thanks to the Duchess, Danby became Jeffreys's friend. The lawyer acted as a spy for the Minister in the City, and he received his reward when he was appointed Solicitor-General to the Duke of York in 1677. Charles never could abide Jeffreys. "That man," he said, "has no learning, no sense, no manners, and more impudence than ten carted street-walkers." But his brother was less shrewd, or perhaps he saw in the young lawyer, with his brazen self-assurance, just the tool and ally that he needed. But, accurately as Charles may have estimated Jeffreys, he was none the less compelled by the Duchess to grant him signal favours. He was knighted in 1677, and in the following year the King and his mistress dined at his house in Buckinghamshire and drank his host's health seven times, and the City, which, for all its independence, was never able to resist the dazzle of royal favour, promptly elected Jeffreys Recorder of London. His first wife conveniently dying at this time, Jeffreys took as his second the daughter of an alderman and "the brisk young widow of a Welsh Knight."

Sitting on the Bench as Recorder, Jeffreys began

to develop the violent invective and monstrous humour for which he is infamous. It was the custom for all the prisoners convicted at the Old Bailey to be sentenced by the Recorder at the end of the Sessions. Macaulay refers to the brutality of one of these addresses. Mr. Irving urges that it was the brutality of the times and not of the man. But the words, as Mr. Irving quotes them, are sufficiently characteristic of Jeffreys's peculiar judicial manner:

And the rest of these women that have the impudence to smoke tobacco and guzzle in alehouses, pretend to buy hoods and scarves only to have an opportunity to steal them, turning thieves to maintain your luxury and pride; so far shall you be from any hope of mercy if we find you here in the future that you shall be sure to have the very rigour of the law inflicted on you. And I charge him that puts the sentence into execution to do it effectually, and particularly to take care of Mrs. Hipkins, scourge her roundly; and the other woman that used to steal gold rings in a country dress; and, since they have a mind to it this cold weather, let them be well heated. Your sentence is that you be taken to the place from whence you came, and from thence be dragged tied to a cart's tail through the streets, your bodies being stripped from the girdle upwards, and be whipt till your bodies bleed.

In sentencing two men convicted for stealing lead from the top of Stepney Church he said: "Your zeal for religion is so great as to carry you to the top of the church. If this be your way of going to church, it is fitting you be taken notice of."

Titus Oates, the Popish plot, and the charges made by that infamous person against the innocent, involved Jeffreys in considerable difficulty. He was in the service of the Duke of York. It was against the Duke of York and his friends that the plots were aimed, and it must be remembered that the fantastic stories would never have been believed but for the wide unpopularity of the Duke and for the fear of the consequences of another Roman Catholic reign. As I have said, the plot brought Danby down, and both the Duchess and the Recorder found a new ally in the intriguing Sunderland. In 1679 it was the Recorder's duty to pass sentence on a number of Jesuits—as he probably

[154]

knew, falsely convicted— -and for once his manner was irreproachable.

During the last four years of Charles's life, Jeffreys was continually briefed by the Crown, and in the trial of one Stephen Colledge, known as "the Protestant joiner," charged with libelling the King in certain pamphlets, Jeffreys had his first personal encounter with Oates, a witness for the defence, whom he deferentially addressed as "doctor," and whom in cross-examination he described as "a witty man and a philosopher." Shortly before this trial, Jeffreys's conduct as Recorder had been the subject of debate in the House of Commons. He was described by Lord William Russell as "a great criminal," and the general opinion of honest men was expressed by one of the Members for Cheshire. It should be said that, among his other judicial offices, Jeffreys was Lord Chief Justice of what was then the County Palatine. The Cheshire representative said:

I cannot be silent as to our chief Judge, and I will name him, because what I have to say will appear more probable: his name is Sir George Jeffreys, who I must say behaved himself more like a jack pudding than with that gravity which beseems a Judge; he was mighty witty upon the prisoners at the bar; he was very full of jokes upon people that came to give evidence, not suffering them to declare what they had to say in their own way and method, but would interrupt them, because they behaved themselves with more gravity than he; and, in truth, the people were strangely perplexed when they were to give their evidence; but I do not insist upon this, nor upon the late hours he kept up and down our city; it's said he was every night drinking till two o'clock, or beyond that time, and that he went to his chamber drunk; but this I have only by common fame, for I was not in his company; I bless God I am not a man of his principles or behaviour; but in the mornings he appeared with the symptoms of a man that over night had taken a large cup. But that which I have to say is the complaint of every man, especially of them who had any lawsuits. Our Chief Justice has a very arbitrary power in appointing the assize when he pleases; and this man has strained it to the highest point; for whereas we were accustomed to have two assizes, the first about April or May, the latter about September, it was this year the middle (as I remember) of August before we had any assize, and then he despatched business so well that he left half the causes untried, and, to help the matter, has resolved that we shall have no more assizes this year.

One Member only spoke for him, and that was his cousin John Trevor, afterwards to be Speaker, and generally known as "squinting Jack." The House petitioned the King to remove Jeffreys from his office, and he himself resigned his Recordership but was permitted to retain the Chief Justiceship of Cheshire. He continued, however, to receive Government briefs, and he was often given precedence of both the Attorney-General and the Solicitor-General. His last important case was the trial of Lord William Russell, in which he summed up the case for the Crown. Russell was accused of complicity in the Rye House plot. No one now supposes that he was guilty. Few even of his political opponents believed in his guilt when he stood for trial. The cautious Evelyn records that there was general pity for Russell "as being thought to have been drawn in on pretence only of endeavouring to rescue the King from his present counsellors and secure religion from Popery and the nation from arbitrary government now so much apprehended." Jeffreys's speech was turgid rather than abusive. He concluded:

[157]

Gentlemen, I must put these things home upon your consciences. I know you will remember the horrid murder of the most pious Prince, the Martyr King Charles the First. How far the practices of those persons have influenced the several punishments since is too great a secret for me to examine. But now I say, you have the life of a merciful King, you have a religion that every honest man ought to stand by, and I am sure every loyal man will venture his life and fortune for. You have *your* wives and children. Let not the greatness of any man corrupt you, but discharge your consciences both to God and the King, and to your posterity.

The trial took place immediately before the long vacation, and at the beginning of the Michaelmas term Jeffreys took his seat in the Court of King's Bench as Lord Chief Justice. Evelyn records that he was "reputed to be most ignorant and most daring," and it was generally understood that the appointment had been made that he might preside at the trial of Algernon Sydney, the most feared of the rebellious Whigs. He opened the trial in characteristic fashion. "Let us have no remarks," he said to the Bar, "but a fair trial in God's name." The only witness against Sydney was Lord Howard of Escrick, described by Evelyn as "that monster of a man," and all through the trial the judge was the prosecutor. He argued with the prisoner with great ingenuity. He contrived to restrain his temper and his language, but at the end, after sentence had been delivered and the prisoner had protested, he snarled at him, "I pray God work in you a temper fit to go into the other world, for I see you are not fit for this." Sydney's execution was unquestionably judicial murder, but, high-minded man as he was, he had stooped to patronise Oates and to use the plots as a political instrument. Without the backing of the Whigs, not a soul would have believed Titus and his friends, and there was something like poetic justice in Sydney's execution.

A few days after the trial, Evelyn met Jeffreys and Wythens, another of the judges, at a wedding. He records that they danced with the bride and were exceeding merry, and he adds: "These great men spent the rest of the afternoon till eleven at night in drinking healths, taking tobacco, and talking much beneath the gravity of judges who had but a day or two before condemned Mr. Algernon Sydney."

Jeffreys was never sure of Charles II. He probably knew that the King disliked him, and the
accession of James II in 1685 promised a considerable acquisition of power and influence. So
excessive was his loyalty that, when the Sheriff's
chaplain at Bedford Assizes, soon after the royal
accession, preached a sermon on Shadrach,
Meshach, and Abednego, who refused to bow the
knee, the Chief Justice, thinking this was a reflec-
tion on his master, was prevented with difficulty
from pulling the preacher out of the pulpit. James
quite properly determined that Oates should not
remain unpunished, but, when he appeared before
Jeffreys in the Court of King's Bench on a charge
of perjury, the judge surprised both his friends
and his enemies by conducting the trial with unusual restraint. He may perhaps have recognised
in Oates some of his own qualities of assurance and
impudence. In his address to the jury his language
was certainly not a whit too strong. He referred
to the "infirmity of the depraved mind, the black-
ness of the soul, the baseness of the actions" of the
prisoner. He called him a "profligate villain" and a

"prostitute monster of impiety," and finally as "the blackest and most perjured villain that ever appeared on the face of the earth"—a perfectly accurate description.

Oates was sentenced to a heavy fine, various pilloryings, and a whipping at the hands of the common hangman from Aldgate to Newgate and afterwards from Newgate to Tyburn. The tough scoundrel survived this brutal treatment, and indeed outlived his judge, from whom he parted, as Mr. Irving suggests and I think is most probable, with mutual understanding and cynical admiration.

As a reward for his conduct of the Oates trial, Jeffreys received a peerage and went to the House of Lords as Baron Jeffreys of Wem in the County of Shropshire. John Churchill was made a peer at the same time. In 1685, Richard Baxter, gentlest of Puritan divines, was arraigned before Jeffreys at the Guildhall for seditious libel on the prelates of the Church of England in his book *Paraphrases of the New Testament*. And at this trial Jeffreys let himself go with a zest. A contemporary has left a piquant account of the proceedings. Pollexfen was the leading counsel for the defence, and the following is part of the proceedings:

Lord C. J. Come, what do you say to that text there? Read it, clerk.

Clerk. Who devour widows' houses, and for a pretence make long prayers, these, etc. (Then the Paraphrase too was read.)

Lord C. J. Oy! Is not this now an old knave to interpret this to be long liturgies?

Pol. So do others of the Church of England, too, my lord, and we are loath to wrong the cause of liturgies as to make them such a novel invention as not to be able to date them as early as the Scribes and Pharisees, etc.

Lord C. J. No, no, Mr. Pollexfen, they were long-winded extemporary prayers, such as they use to say when they appropriate God to themselves, "Lord, we are thy people, thy peculiar people, thy dear people," etc. And then he snorts and speaks through the nose, and clenches his hands and lifts up his goggle eyes in a mimical way, running on furiously, as he saith they used to pray. But old Pollexfen gave him a bite now and then, though he could hardly crowd in a word.

Pol. Why, some will tell you, my lord, it is hard measure to stop these men's mouths and yet not suffer them to speak through the nose.

Lord C. J. Pollexfen, I know you well enough, and I'll set a mark upon you, for you are the patron for the faction. This is an old rogue, and hath poisoned the

[162]

world with his Kidderminster doctrine. Do not we know how he preached formerly. "Curse ye, Meroz, curse them bitterly that come not to help the Lord against the mighty," and encouraged all the women and maids to bring in their bodkins and thimbles to carry on the war against that king of ever-blessed memory; an old schismatical knave, a hypocritical villain!

Pol. I beseech your lordship, suffer me a word for my client. It is well known to all intelligible men of age in this nation, that these things agree not at all to the character of Mr. Baxter, who wished as well to the king and royal family, as Mr. Love that lost his head for endeavouring to bring in the son long before he was restored; and, my lord, Mr. Baxter's loyal and peaceable spirit King Charles II would have rewarded with a bishopric, when he came in, if he could have conformed.

Lord C. J. Oy! Oy! we know that: but what ailed the old stockcole, unthankful villain that he could not conform—was he better or wiser than other men? He hath been ever since the spring of the faction; I am sure he hath poisoned the world with his linsey-wolsey doctrine.

And here I thought he would have run stark staring mad . . . and yet his larum was not run down yet neither; for "he was a conceited, stubborn, fanatical dog, that did not conform when he might have been preferred; hang him! This one old fellow hath cast more reproach upon the constitution and excellent discipline of our Church than will be wiped out this hundred years;

[163]

but I will handle him for it, for, by God! he deserves to be whipped through the city."

Towards the end of the trial the judge addressed the prisoner:

Lord C. J. Come you, what do you say for yourself, you old knave! Come, speak up: what doth he say? I am not afraid of you for all the snivelling calves that are got about you.

Mr. Baxter. Your lordship need not, for I will not hurt you. But these things will surely be understood one day, what tools one sort of Protestants are made to persecute and vex the other. (And lifting up his eyes to heaven said): I am not concerned to answer such stuff, but am ready to produce my writings for the confutation of all this, and my life and conversation is known to many in this nation, etc.

And before the verdict and sentence there was another outburst:

"Richard, Richard, dost thou think we'll hear thee poison the court? Richard, thou art an old fellow, an old knave; thou hast written books enough to load a cart, every one as full of sedition, I might say treason, as an egg is full of meat. Hadst thou been whipped out of thy writing-trade forty years ago, it had been happy. Thou pretendest to be a preacher of the Gospel of Peace,

[164]

and thou hast one foot in the grave: it is time for thee to begin to think what account thou intendest to give. But leave thee to thyself, and I see thou'lt go on as thou hast begun; but, by the grace of God, I'll look after thee."

Baxter was found guilty and fined five hundred marks. The fury of Jeffreys to this mild and saintly scholar with its contrast to the comparative civility to the unspeakable Titus Oates was due to one of the positive passions of Jeffreys's life—his furious hatred of all Dissenters. And after the trial his master disappointed him. James had discovered that it was impossible to gain toleration for Roman Catholics unless toleration was also granted to Dissenters, and he determined to endeavour to arrange an alliance between the two parties. The pardon of Baxter was a step towards this end, but Jeffreys regarded it as a personal affront.

On June 11th, 1685, the Duke of Monmouth landed in Dorsetshire. On July 6th he lost the battle of Sedgemoor, and on July 15th the head-in-air natural son of Charles II was executed for treason on Tower Hill. The West-Country peasants

[165]

paid dearly for their support of Monmouth. They were first handed over to the tender mercies of Colonel Kirke, a ruffian recently returned from commanding in Tangier, who hanged and shot and tortured innocent and guilty with the enthusiasm of a butcher. Kirke used his power in the traditional manner. Forty pounds would buy a man's freedom, and the honour of a pretty wife or daughter. But Kirke was not thorough enough for King James, who was annoyed by the stories of mercy shown to wealthy rebels. It was therefore decided to hold a special western circuit, and, early in September, Jeffreys with four other judges began the Bloody Assize which has covered his name with eternal infamy. Two hundred and fifty rebels were hanged, eight hundred were sold into slavery beyond the sea, at least a thousand were whipped and imprisoned. At Winchester, where the Commission opened, an elderly gentlewoman, Lady Alice Lisle, was accused of harbouring a rebel fugitive. The judge shouted and yelled all through the trial, particularly denouncing the "Presbyterian rascals" whom he loathed. When at the end Lady Alice was convicted and sentenced to death, Jeffreys horrified the jury by saying to them: "If I had been among you and she had been my own mother, I should have found her guilty." Great pressure was brought to bear on the King to grant a reprieve, but he coldly replied that he had left the whole matter to the Lord Chief Justice. Even Churchill, certainly no sentimentalist, was horrified. "This marble," he said striking the chimney-piece with his hand, "is not harder than the King's heart."

From Winchester the judges went on to Salisbury and then to Dorchester, where the Sheriff's chaplain preached a sermon on mercy, and Jeffreys was noticed to laugh grimly. There were three hundred prisoners at Dorchester, and, in order to get through the work, the judge sent word to the prison that a plea of guilty would mean a light sentence, and, although the majority were actually sentenced to death, only ninety-four were hanged. There was only a short list at Exeter, but at Taunton over five hundred prisoners awaited trial. It was from Somerset that Monmouth had drawn most of his recruits, and it was Somerset that paid the bitterest penalty. From Taunton, Jeffreys went to Bristol, where the mayor and aldermen, while not actually joining Monmouth, had been notoriously in sympathy with him. Moreover, they had put themselves outside the law by kidnapping labour for the West Indian estates, in which Bristol was much concerned. Jeffreys harangued them in his best manner. He called them "scoundrel fellows, mere sons of dunghills." He declared: "I find the dirt of the ditch is in your nostrils." The Commission finished its work at Wells, where there were five hundred prisoners, of whom ninety-nine were hanged. It should, perhaps, be said, that most of the people tried by Jeffreys, including Lady Lisle, were technically guilty of treason.

Jeffreys returned to London on September 28th to be received by the King and publicly thanked for his services to the Crown. He had gone straight to Winchester from Tunbridge Wells, where he was taking a cure, and all through the Assize he was suffering agony from a bad attack of stone. Pain brought the worst out of a bad man.

A great deal of money was made during the

Bloody Circuit by the sale of pardons. Even the Queen and her ladies were concerned in the traffic, and Jeffreys for one acquittal received the substantial sum of fifteen thousand pounds, with which he bought a property in the Midlands.

Soon after he returned to London, Jeffreys was made Lord High Chancellor of England. Evelyn writes in his *Diary* under the date October 31st:

I dined at our great Lord Chancellor Jeffreys', who used me with much respect. This was the late Chief-Justice who had newly been to the Western Circuit to try the Monmouth conspirators, and had formerly done such severe justice amongst the obnoxious in Westminster Hall, for which His Majesty dignified him by creating him first a Baron, and now Lord Chancellor. He had some years past been conversant at Deptford; is of an assured and undaunted spirit, and has served the Court interest on all the hardiest occasions; is of nature cruel, and a slave of the Court.

Jeffreys was, as Evelyn says, the slave of a Court intent on its own destruction, though it seems true that he made some feeble protests at James's more extravagant absurdities.

Jeffreys was perhaps the least dignified of all

Lord Chancellors. At one of his dinner parties he engaged an actor to give imitations of the most celebrated lawyers then practising in the courts, and the head of their profession roared with glee. On another occasion Jeffreys and the Lord Treasurer became so drunk that they stripped to their shirts and climbed to the top of a sign-post to drink the health of the King. As this was in January, it is not surprising that the Chancellor was often ill.

In the summer of 1686 Jeffreys was appointed a member of the Ecclesiastical Commission set up by the King with almost unlimited powers. Evelyn says that "it had not only a faculty to inspect and visit all bishops' dioceses, but to change what laws and statutes they should think fit to alter among the colleges though founded by private men; to punish, suspend, fine, etc., give oaths and call witnesses. The main drift was to suppress zealous preachers." The first person cited before the Commission was the Bishop of London, accused of not preventing the Rector of St. Giles's from preaching a controversial sermon. He was found guilty and suspended.

1687 saw the beginning of the end. In April the King granted relief to all Dissenters. Quakers and even Anabaptists were permitted to hold public office, and the Whig City of London promptly elected a Presbyterian as Lord Mayor. In April, too, Jeffreys had the Vice-Chancellor of Cambridge before him for refusing to grant a degree to a Benedictine monk. The Vice-Chancellor was dismissed with the admonition, "Go your way and sin no more!" The Fellows of Magdalen, Oxford, were cited in June, one aged gentleman being terrified when Jeffreys "roared at him like a wild beast." At the beginning of 1688 Jeffreys was very ill. In June the seven bishops were committed to the Tower. Jeffreys warmly protested against the persecution of Sancroft and the others. For what it was worth, he was a Church of England man, and by this time he must have realised that the King was going too far. As Lord Chancellor, of course, he had no connection with the trial or the famous acquittal at Westminster Hall.

On November 5th, 1688, William of Orange landed at Torbay. On December 8th Jeffreys sat for the last time in the Court of Chancery. On the 11th the King fled from Whitehall. Jeffreys was left to shift for himself. He knew his unpopularity. He knew what his fate must be without the protecting arm of the King. He shaved his eyebrows, disguised himself in a sailor's neckcloth and went to Wapping, where he bargained with the captain of a collier for a berth to Hamburg. The boat, however, had to wait for a favourable tide, and one of the crew gave information that a disguised fugitive was anxious to leave the country. Jeffreys, having grown suspicious, had gone ashore and had taken refuge in the Red Cow, in Anchor and Hope Alley, where he was discovered, dirty and in his sailor's disguise, hiding between the blankets of the bed. From Wapping he was taken to Grocers' Hall, surrounded by a furious and howling mob. "There never was such joy," said one observer. Brought before the Lord Mayor, he was committed to the Tower, though the City Magistrate was half fearful of a terrible vegeance, so grim was Jeffreys's reputation.

Jeffreys was forsaken, hopeless, and extremely

ill. Two bishops came to see him and some of his enemies called to jeer. He was tortured with stone and rheumatism. He could eat nothing, and on April 18th, 1689, he died, having first made a will in which he professed his undiminished allegiance to the Church of England. "I do charge all my children," he wrote, "upon the blessing of a dying father they be steady to the commands I have given them of being firm even to death to the principles of that holy Church." What those principles were it would probably have been difficult for Jeffreys to have explained. The name of God was frequently on his lips. The fear of God could hardly have been in his heart.

MARLBOROUGH

JOHN CHURCHILL
1650–1722

MARLBOROUGH

JOHN CHURCHILL, first Duke of Marlborough, was a supreme master of the art of war and the greatest general in English history. At the head of an allied army in which there were never more than fourteen thousand English troops, and over which his supreme command was always challenged, he won the victories of Blenheim, Ramillies, Oudenarde, and Malplaquet in the course of an extended campaign that lasted for eight years. For the first time for three hundred years a British general and a British army had been successful on the continent of Europe, and in those eight years Marlborough broke the power of France. He is conspicuous among great military leaders for the consideration that he always showed to the men under his command, and it has been said of him that he "secured the affection of his soldiers by his good nature, his care for their provisions, and vigilance not to expose them to unnecessary danger."

He saw that his soldiers were properly fed. He saw that they were promptly paid. His own calmness and serenity in battle were an inspiration. "Our Duke," says Thackeray in *Esmond*, "was as calm at the mouth of a cannon as at the door of a drawing-room."

Marlborough had all the domestic virtues. His wife, the famous Sarah, was a termagant of the worst description, but he was a fond and faithful husband and a most affectionate father.

Marlborough's genius as a soldier was matched by his skill as a diplomatist. Without his supreme diplomacy, the alliance against France would never have held together, and the advantages of the Peace of Utrecht would never have been obtained.

It is one of the tragedies of history that this great figure should be besmirched by treachery, meanness, and greed, perhaps exaggerated by Macaulay, to whom want of fidelity to Dutch William was the unforgivable sin, but which so fervent an admirer as Mr. Saintsbury is compelled to admit and tries unsuccessfully to explain away. Thackeray painted Marlborough as inhuman in his cold detachment from those moral considerations which affect the actions of lesser men. He says:

He performed a treason or a court-bow, he told a falsehood as black as Styx, as easily as he paid a compliment or spoke about the weather. He took a mistress, and left her; he betrayed his benefactor, and supported him, or would have murdered him, with the same calmness always, and having no more remorse than Clotho when she weaves the thread, or Lachesis when she cuts it. . . . He achieved the highest deed of daring, or deepest calculation of thought, as he performed the very meanest action of which a man is capable; told a lie, or cheated a fond woman, or robbed a poor beggar of a halfpenny, with a like awful serenity and equal capacity of the highest and lowest acts of our nature.

The picture is over-coloured, and Macaulay exaggerates with even greater enthusiasm. Mr. Saintsbury scornfully summarises the charges:

Venal without hesitation or limit; shamelessly and indifferently treacherous; not indeed wantonly cruel, but as careless of others' blood as of his own honour when his interest was concerned; faithless to his party; trimming to the end between the rival claimants to the crown; sordidly avaricious; such is the portrait of Marlborough that we are often asked to accept.

[179]

Prejudice may have summarised his career as "a prodigy of turpitude," but unpleasant vices certainly besmirch unchallengeable greatness.

Marlborough's honour, indeed, was rooted in dishonour. He was the son of Winston Churchill, a Dorsetshire country gentleman, and was born in 1650. He was educated at St. Paul's School, and when he was fifteen he became page to the Duke of York, afterwards James II. He obtained this engagement through the influence of his sister Arabella, whom Count Grammont mercilessly describes as "a tall creature, pale-faced and nothing but skin and bone," who was one of James's mistresses, and afterwards the mother of his son the Duke of Berwick, a gallant soldier who fought against his uncle Marlborough in many engagements, and proved himself, illegitimate though he was, by far the best Stuart of them all. Churchill owed his start in life to his sister's dishonourable distinction, and he owed his first preferment to the fact that the Duchess of Cleveland, mistress of King Charles and a woman many years his senior, fell in love with him. Grammont tells us that "all agreed that a man who was the favourite of the King's mistress and brother to the Duke's favourite was in a fair way to preferment and could not fail to make his fortune." The Duchess of Cleveland gave Marlborough a present of five thousand pounds, with which he bought himself an annuity —a rare example of prudence and foresight in a young man not yet out of his teens.

When Churchill was seventeen he received a commission in the Guards and served for a time at Tangier, and in 1672 he went to France with the troops that Charles II sent to aid Louis XIV in the conquest of Holland, in fulfilment of a most dishonourable agreement. Even as a junior officer, Churchill's talents were sufficient to attract the notice and the praise of the great Turenne. In 1678, Marlborough married Sarah Jennings, the younger sister of Frances Jennings, a famous Restoration beauty, who was exactly ten years his junior. Never was a great man more uxorious; rarely has a great man suffered the tantrums of a violent-tempered woman with such exemplary patience. Mr. Saintsbury, always the eager apologist of the husband, has no good word for the wife. She was, he says, without a spark of honour, gratitude, patriotism, decency, or moderation, and she was a curse to her family. Her only virtue was that she was not a hypocrite.

Churchill married his wife for love, and remained in love with her all his life. Nearly five and twenty years afterwards he wrote to her:

It is impossible to express with what a heavy heart I parted with you when I was by the water's side. I could have given my life to come back, though I knew my own weakness so much that I durst not, for I know I should have exposed myself to the company. I did for a great while, with a perspective glass, look upon the cliffs, in hopes I might have had one sight of you. We are now out of sight of Margate, and I have neither soul nor spirits, but I do at this moment suffer so much that nothing but being with you can recompense it. If you will be sensible of what I now feel, you will endeavour ever to be easy to me, and then I shall be most happy: for it is you only that can give me true content. I pray God to make you and yours happy: and if I could contribute anything to it with the utmost hazard of my life, I should be glad to do it.

His terror of his wife's moods is again indicated in a letter that he wrote after the victory of Malplaquet, in which he says, "Nothing in this world can make me happy if you are not kind."

After their marriage, Churchill and his wife were attached to the household of the Duke and Duchess of York, and in 1682 he was created Baron Churchill and given the command of a Dragoon regiment. At the accession of James II, Churchill was not forgotten. He received part of the considerable money present sent to James by Louis, and went to Paris to convey the King's thanks for a gift dictated by policy and accepted by a prince without dignity or self-respect. Churchill may have anticipated, from his knowledge of the character of James, that his reign would be brief and stormy, and he is said to have declared that "if the King should attempt to change our religion and constitution, I will instantly quit his service." He was largely responsible for the defeat of Monmouth at Sedgemoor, but he had no sort of responsibility for the bloodthirsty revenge inflicted on the Somerset peasants who had joined the Pretender's army. After Sedgemoor, Marlborough and his wife, again probably disliking and fearing the King's policy,

[183]

absented themselves from Court and attached themselves to Princess Anne, the King's second daughter by his first wife, with whom Lady Churchill had already established the intimate friendship that lasted for years and which she was so blatantly to abuse. The Princess was estranged from her father after the birth of the Prince of Wales. She was sincerely attached to the Church of England, and, if she was not privy to the conspiracy that brought William of Orange to England, she certainly preferred her sister and brother-in-law to her father and stepmother.

Churchill's part in the revolution was mean and disgraceful. He was among the politicians who treated with William, but despite this fact, he accepted the command of the troops sent to oppose the Dutch Prince's landing. In the night, while camped outside Salisbury, he stole away and deserted to the enemy. The desertion was a little too much even for William's friends, and old Schomberg bluntly told the traitor that it was the first time in history that an officer of his rank had deserted the colours. It is said, by way of excuse, that

Churchill was at least fervent and honest in his devotion to the Church of England. In a vindication of her husband, Sarah said: "It was evident to all the world that, as things were carried on by James, everybody sooner or later must be ruined who would not become a Roman Catholic." And in this Sarah completely gives her husband away. He had retained the confidence of James until the last moment. He had timed his desertion so that the King's army was left leaderless before its enemy because he was convinced that he must either change his religion or lose his fortune. I am inclined to regard all Macaulay's judgments with considerable suspicion, but there is certainly reasonable justification for his indictment:

The earthly evil which he most dreaded was poverty. The one crime from which his heart recoiled was apostasy. And if the designs of the Court succeeded, he could not doubt that between poverty and apostasy he must soon make his choice. He therefore determined to cross those designs; and it soon appeared that there was no guilt and no disgrace which he was not ready to incur in order to escape from the necessity of parting either with his places or with his religion.

Before his desertion, Churchill wrote James a letter reeking with suave hypocrisy. It was as follows:

SIR,—Since men are seldom suspected of sincerity, when they act contrary to their interests, and though my dutiful behaviour to your Majesty in the worst of times (for which I acknowledge my poor services much overpaid) may not be sufficient to incline you to a charitable interpretation of my actions, yet I hope the great advantage I enjoy under your Majesty, which I can never expect in any other change of government, may reasonably convince your Majesty and the world that I am actuated by a higher principle, when I offer that violence to my inclination and interest as to desert your Majesty at a time when your affairs seem to challenge the strictest obedience from all your subjects, much more from one who lies under the greatest obligations to your Majesty. This, Sir, could proceed from nothing but the inviolable dictates of my conscience and a necessary concern for my religion (which no good man can oppose), and with which I am instructed nothing can come in competition. Heaven knows with what partiality my dutiful opinion of your Majesty has hitherto represented those unhappy designs which inconsiderate and self-interested men have framed against your Majesty's true interest and the Protestant religion; but as I can no longer join with such to give a pretence by conquest to bring them to effect, so I will always, with the hazard of

[186]

my life and fortune (so much your Majesty's due) endeavour to preserve your royal person and lawful rights, with all the tender concerns and dutiful respect that become, Sir, your Majesty's most dutiful and most obliged subject and servant.

It is true, of course, that Churchill was only one among many traitors, though no other man timed his treachery so astutely. It is true also that a man must be judged by the moral standard of his time and not by the moral standard of later ages. Much has been made of Churchill's devotion to the Church of England. Mr. Saintsbury says that he was a man of "a definite and strong religious faith bound by that fidelity to a certain form of Church doctrine and government." Macaulay acknowledges his devotion to his Church. Thackeray emphasises the reality of his religion. "Before his actions he always had the Church service read solemnly and professed an undoubting belief that our Queen's arms were blessed and our victory sure." I am unconvinced. What could be astuter than for a general to persuade his soldiers that they are armed with the sword of the Lord and of

Gideon? And it is surely probable that it was not fear of apostasy that caused the Churchills to desert James and to join William, but the conviction that James was certain to be beaten and that William was certain to become King of England. Wisdom dictated the change over to the winning side.

Treachery had its reward. In April 1689, William made Churchill Earl of Marlborough, but the King's Dutch confidant, Bentinck, afterwards Earl of Portland, disliked and distrusted him, and the King properly feared the man who had betrayed his father-in-law at the eleventh hour. Marlborough, however, was given employment. He was first sent to the Netherlands; and, after the Battle of the Boyne, he led a successful expedition to the south of Ireland, where for the first time he had a real opportunity of displaying his outstanding military abilities.

No sooner was William in London, and James settled in exile in Saint-Germain, than Marlborough began underhand negotiations with his old master and against the new. In this he was following popular sentiment and the example of a considerable number of the statesmen who had sworn allegiance to the Dutch King. England hated being ruled by a foreigner. The King was *gauche*. The presence in England of Dutch soldiers and politicians was resented. The misdoings of the Stuarts were forgotten now that they were in exile. It would not have been difficult, if James had had a rudimentary idea of politics and English politicians could have been persuaded to have been consistent in their treachery, to have compelled William hurriedly to return to the Hague in the early years of his reign. But James was a fool and William was astute, and, with places and favour, semi-loyalty was secured from Marlborough, and the communications with Saint-Germain came to an end for the time. The blackest example of treachery of which Marlborough was guilty before he was bought was to betray the details of a proposed English expedition to Brest, with the idea, of course, that James should carry his knowledge to the French King. The expedition was a complete failure, with over a thousand casualties, and the death and suffering, for which Marlborough was responsible, can hardly be attributed to his devotion to the Protestant religion.

In May 1692, Marlborough was disgraced. His plottings had apparently been unsuspected by even his well-informed contemporaries, for, writing in his *Diary* on February 28th, 1692, Evelyn says: "Lord Marlborough having used words against the King, and being discharged from all his great places, his wife was forbid the Court, and the Princess of Denmark was desired by the Queen to dismiss her from her service; she refusing to do so goes away from Court to Syon-House."

Mary always disliked the Marlboroughs—much more, indeed, than her husband—and the quarrel between her and her sister Anne to which Evelyn refers lasted till Mary's death. The partial reconciliation that took place between the King and Marlborough after the death of the Queen was due to William's conviction that the Duke was the one man in England with the will and the ability to carry on his anti-French policy.

William of Orange, and Marlborough after him, were obsessed by the balance of power, and not unnaturally. At the end of the seventeenth century the France of Louis XIV had acquired a European dominance only to be challenged by a continental alliance, a dominance that threatened the liberties and independence of the Netherlands, which William loved, and of England, which he used.

Louis XIV ascended the French throne in 1643, and the peace of Ryswick was signed in 1697. In fifty years he had added to the dominions that he had inherited a large part of Alsace, with the city of Strasbourg, the towns of Toul and Verdun, with Metz and part of Lorraine. He had acquired from the Spanish Netherlands the province of Artois, with its many flourishing towns, including Arras, St. Omer, Bapaume, and Lens, and also the important fortified cities of Lille, Tournai, and Charleroi. On the east, Franche-Comté was incorporated in France. The Spaniards had been driven out of the territory which they had held north of the Pyrenees, and France had acquired important possessions in the north of Italy. As Mr. Frank Taylor said: "In a period of fifty years an able, arrogant, and unscrupulous diplomacy, supported always by war in its most relentless form, had girdled her (France) with fortresses and carried her borders to the Pyrenees, the Alps, and the Vosges. Herself immune from attack, she could issue forth at will into the valleys of the Scheldt, the Meuse, the Rhine, the Ebro and the Po."

In his years of successful fighting and astute diplomacy, Marlborough was certainly, according to his lights, playing the part of an English patriot, and maybe of a good European. But he was not without the personal ambition of the successful soldier, and for all his realism he was affected by that yearning for "glory" which has wrought so much misery for the workaday world and hurried hundreds and thousands of men into a premature grave. This is shown in a letter that he wrote to his wife on October 26th, 1704:

This march and my own spleen have given me occasion to think how very unaccountable a creature man is, to be seeking for honour in so barren a country as this, when he is very sure that the greater part of mankind, and may justly fear that even his best friends, would be apt to think ill of him should he have ill success.

Thanks to the mole in the grounds of Hampton Court, William died in 1702 and was succeeded by Queen Anne, and her accession meant a great change in the Marlboroughs' fortune. He was made a Knight of the Garter; his wife was made Ranger of Windsor Forest; and, two months after the Queen's accession, Marlborough was appointed Commander-in-Chief of the allied armies operating against the French. Then followed his triumphs, achieved, as I have said, in the face of most tremendous difficulties. Liège was captured in December 1702, and Marlborough was made a Duke. Blenheim was fought and won in 1704, and the Queen gave Marlborough the manor of Woodstock and began to spend the quarter of a million of money which it cost to build Blenheim Palace for him and his descendants. Ramillies was won in 1706, and practically the whole of the Low Countries were recovered from the French. Oudenarde was won in 1708, and the city of Lille captured. Malplaquet was won in 1709, and the campaigns were brought to an end by the Treaty of Utrecht, signed in 1713.

Victory and triumph left Marlborough's charm

of manner unimpaired. Evelyn, then in his eighty-fifth year, met Marlborough in London soon after the victory of Blenheim. "I went to wait on my Lord Treasurer," he says, "where was the victorious Duke of Marlborough who came to me and took me by the hand with extraordinary familiarity and civility, as formerly he was used to do, without any alteration of his good nature. He had a most rich George in a sardonyx set with diamonds of very great value; for the rest very plain. I had not seen him for some years and believed he might have forgotten me."

Before the Peace of Utrecht was signed the great general was disgraced. In 1710 the Whig Ministries that had supported the war, and with which Marlborough was allied, were succeeded by a Tory administration, with Harley and St. John at its head and Swift as its principal pamphleteer. The country was weary of war and resentful of the profits that Marlborough had made out of the war, while the Queen was wearier still of his wife. To a large extent Marlborough owed no allegiance to any political party, though he was constantly concerned in political intrigue. If anything, he was a mild Tory, but Sarah was an enthusiastic and venomous Whig, and it was her Whiggery more than anything else that caused her rupture with the Queen. With his matchless vigour, Swift demanded peace in pamphlet after pamphlet, and Marlborough blundered badly. Both Harley and St. John were more than ready to treat with him. His prestige was unchallenged. But he threw away every advantage that he possessed by advocating a policy of war at any price and assuming a partisan and unpatriotic hostility to the Government.

In the *Examiner*, Swift drew up two tables comparing the rewards of a Roman and of a British general. The Roman in all cost his country £994 11s. 10 *d.*, including twopence for a crown of laurel. The British general had cost his country £540,000. In 1706 another calculation gave Marlborough a yearly income of £62,325 in salaries, gifts, allowances, and commissions. In the autumn of 1711 he was publicly accused of receiving £70,000 from a Jewish army contractor and of deducting two and a half per cent. from the pay of

[195]

the foreign soldiers in the English service, and the Queen dismissed him from all employment. It is probable, as Mr Saintsbury suggests, that the charges made against him were mere pretexts. The truth was that, while he was in power, peace was impossible. The Duchess's disgrace had preceded that of her husband. She was ordered to leave her apartments in St. James's Palace, and she was so angry that she tore down the mantelpieces and stole the brass locks from the doors. After his disgrace, Marlborough, now a man of sixty-two, weary, disappointed, and resentful, went to the Continent, where he stayed to the end of Anne's reign. It was characteristic of him that before he left England he invested £50,000 in Holland, in order to secure an income if the Stuarts regained the English crown.

While he was successfully fighting against the French, Marlborough was persistently negotiating with the Stuarts through his nephew, the Duke of Berwick, and as early as 1703 it had been suggested that the unhappy prince, known as the Old Pretender, should marry one of Marlborough's daughters. During these two years of exile he was in constant communication with the Elector of Hanover, destined to be Anne's successor if the Protestant succession was maintained, as well as with the Stuarts. It is, of course, notorious that before her death, and possibly owing to the influence of St. John, Anne herself became a fervent Jacobite, and that, had it been possible, she would have secured the throne for her half-brother, and it was perhaps his anger at Anne's conduct to him that induced Marlborough to intrigue with Hanover. But the Elector George was a very astute gentleman, with a keen appreciation of how far Marlborough was to be trusted. He was ready enough to make use of him, but he appears to have been well aware that Marlborough was plotting with Saint Germain as well as with him. The truth was that the English wanted neither a Roman Catholic nor a German king. It was a choice of evils. While Anne was dying, it was obvious that the fate of the English throne depended on whether Charles or George was able to arrive first in London. Marlborough contrived to reach London on the day after the Queen's death. But he was too late. George had spent his money wisely, and had secured sufficient support to make the succession certain without Marlborough's aid. The duke was among the notables who met the new king at Greenwich, and was confirmed in the appointments that he had held under Queen Anne. But his public career was over. His life was saddened by the death of his daughters, and, according to Johnson, he fell into a premature dotage. He played with his grandchildren; he endured his wife's temper, which ever grew worse, with exemplary patience; and he died on June 16th, 1722.

Marlborough had many fine qualities. Comparing him with Cromwell and Wellington, the two other men of military genius that England has produced in modern times, Mr. Fortescue says: "All three were endowed with strong character, striking moral and physical courage, indefatigable industry, and that combination of penetrating insight and transcendant common sense which is called originality. All three commanded the utmost confidence of their subordinates; but Marlborough alone of them possessed the mysterious gift of personal charm. It is this which makes his career of such surpassing interest." It was this quality, too, which enabled him to endure and conquer Dutch obstinacy and to placate arrogant kings.

I have spoken of his family affection. His life was not without an ample share of anxieties and disappointments, but the bitterest of his experiences was the death from smallpox of his seventeen years old son. Sarah, generally a hard self-seeker, was absolutely heartbroken, and for months suffered from a melancholy that threatened to become insanity. Marlborough was dignified in his deep sorrow, and, since no man can play the hypocrite when his heart is broken, the letter that he wrote to his wife may be taken as incontrovertible evidence that his religion, often useful as a pretext, was not without its reality:

You and I have great reason to bless God for all we have, so that we must not repine at His taking our poor child from us, but bless and praise Him for what His goodness leaves us. . . . The use I think we should make of this His correction is, that our chiefest time should be spent in reconciling ourselves to Him, and having in our minds always that we may not have long to live in this world.

His will was indomitable. He was very ill after Blenheim, and was threatened with consumption, but he refused to go home. The military situation was perilous, and no one but he could cope with its difficulties. "Neither vexation of spirit," says Mr. Taylor, "nor bodily infirmity, nor the remonstrances of those he loved, could turn him from his project."

Marlborough had good looks, personal charm, and attractive manners. Chesterfield declared that "he possessed the graces in the highest degree." As Evelyn has testified, he was charmingly pleasant to old age. He plotted and intrigued, but always with an air. Of many things with which he was charged he was guiltless. In many of his meannesses he was no better and no worse than the majority of his contemporaries. As a soldier he cared nothing for show, and only occasionally for glory. At the head of his armies he was a practical man of affairs, never wasting men unnecessarily, never depressed by difficulty or over-elated by success.

But the greatness of the man was marred and spoiled and made ugly by a covetousness and an avariciousness hardly to be matched in the life-stories of men distinguished among their fellows. He lied and plotted and betrayed, he fought and won, always with an eye on his bank balance, always in the hope of adding to his possessions.

FREDERICK THE GREAT

FREDERICK II
1712–1786

FREDERICK THE GREAT

FREDERICK THE GREAT of Prussia is one of the great blackguards of history. That Carlyle found in him qualities to admire must be ascribed to the inevitable eccentricity of a Scottish philosopher. Lord Acton has called Frederick a "consummate practical genius," and certainly no ruler has ever known better how to exploit the tangled circumstances of his time and to derive the greatest personal advantage from both victory and defeat. In his youth Frederick was the author of an essay in which he criticised the political principles of Machiavelli, but not even Thomas Cromwell was a more constant disciple of the Italian philosopher. He accepted to the full the theory of Louis XIV that the State was the King and that the King could do no wrong. Men might therefore quite properly lie, murder, and plot to secure advantage for the State—that is, for the King—even though they might hesitate to lie, murder, and plot for themselves. It was a theory generally accepted in the eighteenth century, and it is a theory by no means repudiated in the twentieth century, though the belief that the State is the King is no longer accepted.

Personally, Frederick was offensive in manner and appearance. His clothes were habitually shabby and covered with snuff. He hardly ever washed even his hands and face, and a particularly unpleasant aspect of the man is suggested by the fact that his dirty face, with its badly clipped beard, was generally touched up with paint. He enjoyed petty cruelty and vulgar insults. He was a coward, who, on more than one occasion during the Seven Years' War, fled in terror from the battlefield when it was clear that his army had lost. His joy in cruelty was shown by the order that he gave during the campaign against Russia in 1757 that no prisoners should be taken and that the enemy wounded should be killed. His mean dishonesty was shown by his method of raising money by debasing the coinage, in which nefarious little plan he obtained the help of three Jewish experts.

He was immensely industrious and was fond of

describing himself as "the servant of the State," but never once in his reign did he prefer the interests of his people to mere selfish considerations. His interest in philosophy and the philosophers, so characteristic of the eighteenth century, was a royal pastime and not to be regarded as evidence of either originality or acute intelligence.

"It is a prominent principle among princes," he once wrote, "to aggrandise themselves as much as they can." That was his policy. His success was gained by consistent hypocrisy and fraud. In international affairs he was, in Mr. Norwood Young's phrase, "the polite highwayman."

The Hohenzollerns are parvenus among the royal families of Europe. In 1412, Frederick Hohenzollern, Burgrave of Nuremberg, conquered Brandenburg, a harsh, marshy province at the mouth of the Elbe, and was recognised by the Emperor as one of the seven German Electors. The Hohenzollerns remained in the marsh, pompous princes of second-rate importance, until the middle of the sixteenth century, when East Prussia was added to their territory. In 1640, Frederick Wil-

liam, the first of the family of any importance, succeeded to the Electorate. Germany had been laid
waste by the Thirty Years' War. In 1648 the Peace
of Westphalia robbed the Emperor of almost all
his authority in the outer Marches. It was the ideal
opportunity for an ambitious Protestant prince to
extend his dominions.

Frederick William raised an army largely by kidnapping in adjacent territories. He collected funds
by crushing his people with excessive taxation. He
dealt mercilessly with all opposition. He became a
personage, no small achievement when it is remembered that, in the middle of the seventeenth century, the Hohenzollerns, who were to become the
idols of Prussia, were still regarded by the Prussians as interloping foreigners. By aiding Sweden
against the Poles and afterwards by aiding Poland
against Sweden, and by a series of other bewildering alliances during the next twenty years, Frederick William, the Great Elector, established the
Hohenzollerns in Berlin as a power to be reckoned
with. When he died, Hohenzollern despotism was
established, backed by the first standing army in

modern Europe. It should be added that, like his great grandson, the Great Elector was a first-class cheat and liar.

His son, Frederick, the first King of Prussia, married Sophia Charlotte, sister of George I. The prestige of this alliance secured for him from the Emperor permission to call himself the King of Prussia, a permission only given because Prussia was a small, poor, and inconsiderable province, and its King, so it was supposed, could have no European importance. Frederick was succeeded in 1713 by his son, Frederick William, a frugal and heavy-drinking person whose principal amusement was the collection of very tall soldiers. He collected them as other men collect stamps, not for use, but in order that he might have the pleasure of looking at them. He sent his recruiting officers throughout Europe, buying the giants for whom he had so great a passion that he would never make war for fear that some of these large and cherished persons might unfortunately be killed. The tall soldiers were Frederick William's only extravagance. In other respects, never was there so parsimonious a monarch.

Though Frederick William had no thought for the happiness of his subjects, his economies were immensely useful to the State. Waste land was reclaimed, roads were made, schools were built.

The King was naïve and entirely uncultured, and the greater part of his day was spent drinking beer and smoking clay pipes with his friends. His idea of humour was to invite learned men to his table and to make them drunk. He may perhaps be best described as unpleasantly simple.

Frederick, his only son, was born in 1712. In every respect he was the antithesis of his father. Frederick William was a pious Protestant. Frederick from his early youth laughed at religion. Frederick William loved rowdy songs. His son preferred to play delicate tunes on the flute. The father was a typical German. The son, all through his life, professed scorn for his own people, preferring to speak French and loving to ape the manners of the Court of Versailles. The father was a boor. The son was a pedant and a prig.

Frederick's youth was unhappy. Life, indeed, can rarely have been very happy in an eighteenth-century German Court. His father hated him, resenting his effeminacy, and subjected him to every possible humiliation. On more than one occasion he thrashed him in public, even when he was adolescent. Frederick in his turn not unnaturally hated his father, but his letters to him are full of such hypocritical snivellings as:

> I beg my dear Papa to be gracious to me, and I can after long reflection assert that my conscience has not accused me in the slightest degree of anything as to which I should reproach myself; but if I should, against my will and intention, have done anything to vex my dear Papa, I herewith most submissively beg for forgiveness.

In 1732, Frederick was married by his father's orders to the Princess Elizabeth Christina of Brunswick. Women never had the smallest attraction for him. He lived with his wife for four years, mainly because he preferred her society to his father's, but he never saw her after his accession to the throne. Soon after his son's marriage, the King had a bad attack of dropsy and was not expected to live. Frederick cried his heart out at his father's side. He was always an adept at weeping. But when his father recovered, he was furious. He wrote to his sister Wilhelminah: "You may consider, my very dear sister, that thanks to God he has the constitution of a Turk and that he will survive his posterity if he so desires and if he takes care of himself."

It was in the years after his marriage and before his accession that Frederick began to correspond with Voltaire, to whom he was attracted because he was both a Frenchman and a philosopher. His favourite amusement was writing bad French verse, and, in imitation of fashionable French scepticism, he proclaimed himself an unbeliever. Voltaire's letters to the Prussian prince lacked nothing in fulsomeness, though he ventured to point out to the budding poet that *trompette* does not rhyme with *tête*, adding, with his tongue in his cheek, that, if the Prince would pay attention to small details, he would assuredly become a member of the Académie Française. The grateful Prince addressed the philosopher as "divine Aristotle" and "divine Plato,"

[212]

and elaborated to him his theories of God and the universe. It was at this time that Frederick wrote the essay on Machiavelli to which I have already referred, and even Voltaire suggested that the treatise was rather long. It is typical in its hypocrisy. Machiavelli was too candid for Frederick. He said what he thought. The Prince, himself, was—I quote Mr. Norwood Young—"a secret and furtive Machiavelli."

Frederick William died on May 31st, 1740, and at the age of twenty-eight his son became the third Hohenzollern King of Prussia. In the same year, the Emperor Charles VI died, to be succeeded by his daughter, the unlucky Maria Theresa. Her right was acknowledged by the agreement known as the Pragmatic Sanction, but she was not permitted to use the title of Empress. Her succession weakened the power of the Empire and was an obvious temptation to Hohenzollern ambition, particularly as her position was challenged by the Bavarian house of Wittelsbach.

If Frederick benefited from the weakness of one woman, he found in the early years of his reign the most persistent and successful opposition from another woman, the Empress Elizabeth of Russia, the daughter of Peter the Great, who succeeded her cousin Anne, a mountain of a woman, grim and sensual, in 1741. For twenty years Elizabeth barred the way to Prussian conquest. She was a politician of the very first rank, and, when Frederick heard of her death, he not unnaturally exclaimed, "The sky begins to clear."

Louis XV had succeeded to the throne of France in 1715, destined to reap what his great-grandfather had sown. His reign was a reign of disaster. The Battle of Plassey in 1757 and the Battle of the Heights of Abraham in 1759 were two events of immense significance in the history of Europe. They made England, and not France, the dominant power in India and North America. They discredited the Bourbons, and they made middle-class France determined on a revolutionary change of government. The English victories in India and Canada were, to a large extent, made possible by Pitt's juggling of European alliances against France, and since these intrigues centred round the unwashed, painted sovereign in Berlin, he may be well regarded as one of the chief actors in the prologue of the drama that began at Versailles in 1789.

Frederick had hardly been crowned King of Prussia when he began his highwayman career. He had inherited from his father an army of ninety thousand men, an immense number when it is remembered that the whole population of his territories was only two and a quarter millions. But more than half the army had been recruited outside Prussia. Frederick William loved an army for ornament. His son was eager to use it, and, with a preliminary campaign of lies to Maria Theresa and to George I, Frederick led his army into Silesia, then an Austrian province, which he declared belonged by right to his house. The Prussian and Austrian armies met at Mollwitz in an indecisive battle. Frederick, however, feared that the onslaught of the Austrian cavalry could not be resisted by his Prussian infantry, and galloped from the battlefield before the fight was half over. His cowardice has been well compared with the pluck of fat little George II at the battle of Dettingen.

All through his reign Frederick was the child of good fortune, and even the battle of Mollwitz added to his prestige. It suggested that the dismemberment of the overgrown Austrian Empire was possible, and other nations were at once hungry for their share in the spoil. France made a treaty with Prussia against Maria Theresa, and two French armies crossed the Rhine. This was the beginning of a campaign that, with many interludes of dishonest negotiations, continued until 1745. The Treaty of Dresden, signed in this year, gave Silesia to Prussia, and Frederick returned to Berlin at the end of 1745 to be acclaimed a conqueror.

For eleven years Prussia was at peace mainly owing to the fact that the watchful, long-headed Elizabeth was still reigning in Moscow, and Frederick had time to build his Versailles at Potsdam. The gardens of Sans-Souci were garnished with trees cut in the shapes of men and sausages. The palace, little more than a villa, was decorated with sculptured cupids. The Prussian Versailles was bizarre and vulgar. The Queen was never admitted to Sans-Souci. She was, indeed, treated by her husband with heartless indifference. When her brother was killed fighting in Frederick's army, he protested that it was his own fault, and that he wondered that he had not been killed long before. Indifference and neglect were borne with dignified patience. "I have nothing to reproach myself with," the Queen wrote, "and I do my duty. The good God will help me to bear this with many other things."

The Court at Sans-Souci mainly consisted of cosmopolitan literary men of the second and third order whom the King alternately patronised and bullied, and most of whom were glad to escape from his unpleasant society after a very few months. Frederick's peculiar humour was shown on one occasion when the Marquis d'Agens was extremely ill. The King disguised himself as a priest, took with him sacred vessels stolen from a church, and with acolytes by his side gave the sick man Extreme Unction!

In the summer of 1750, Voltaire came to Sans-Souci. He had met the King four times before—two of his visits to Germany having been semi-official diplomatic missions—and he certainly had no illusions concerning his character. "I would rather," he wrote in 1743, "live in a Swiss village than enjoy the dangerous favour of a king who is capable of importing treason even into friendship." It was therefore with his eyes open that Voltaire went to Potsdam. On his side Frederick was perfectly candid. "One may learn good things from a criminal," he wrote. "I desire to learn his French. What need I care about his morality?"

Voltaire was lonely and unhappy. Madame du Châtelet had died in 1749 and he wanted change. He was received with royal favours, decorated with the Order of Merit, and promised a considerable salary. At first he was happy enough, but before the end of the year he grew uncomfortable. Voltaire caused the King reasonable annoyance by a very doubtful deal in Saxon banknotes, and in a grovelling letter implored forgiveness. The incident is the severest criticism of Voltaire's character, and all the details of his stay at Potsdam reflect much more on him than on the Prussian King. Voltaire at Potsdam was at his worst and meanest. Frederick was just himself. In 1751 he declared, "I shall have need of him for another year at most. When the orange has been squeezed, the skin is thrown away."

Voltaire grew weary at last of correcting the royal doggerel verse. "How much longer," he exclaimed, "must I go on washing his dirty linen?" But he stayed on, hoping that he would at least take back from Germany a considerable competence. And in this he was disappointed. The parting was bitter. Voltaire tried to trick the King and failed, and he only succeeded in reaching safety and quiet in Switzerland after a world of humiliation. The experience was not without its value. Voltaire had seen tyranny at first hand. He had experienced the pettiness of the tyrant, and his sympathy with misfortune was intensified. He was well over fifty when he went to Potsdam. It was nearly forty years later when his bones were taken from their sepulture in the Abbey of Sellières and were placed beside those of Mirabeau in the Panthéon, the procession consisting of "cars drawn by eight white horses, goadsters in classical costumes with fillets and wheat ears enough." The friend of the king, who despised mankind, had become in his death the idol of the Revolution, intended to establish the rights of mankind.

There was, indeed, nothing in common between Frederick and Voltaire except perhaps their scepticism. But although Voltaire may not have believed in the Christian God, he believed in some sort of God, and had at least some of Rousseau's belief in man. For Frederick, man was a brute to be treated like a brute, and this innate wickedness of man justified wars and the tyranny of rulers. "The more I know man," he once said, "the more I like dogs."

The era of peace came to an end in 1756. While nominally at peace in Europe, the French and English colonists were, as has been said, fighting for supremacy in the American colonies, and the idea occurred to the ministers of Maria Theresa that the hostility between the Western powers might be utilised to recover Silesia. The first step was to persuade France into an alliance which would act as a counterpoise if Great Britain were to support Prussia. The idea was explained to Madame de Pompadour—who not only ruled Louis

XV, but practically controlled the French Government—and appealed to her hazy statesmanship. Having secured the support of France, Austria turned to Russia. The Empress Elizabeth was always suspicious of Frederick and needed little persuasion to join a league against him. Indeed, she was so eager for hostile action that she was with difficulty persuaded to remain inactive until the whole Austrian plan could be completed.

Frederick was well served by his spies, and was at once acquainted with the enemy's plans. A loosely worded treaty with England was signed in January 1756, and, four months afterwards, war which began badly for England was declared between England and France. It was Pitt's plan so to embroil France in Europe that she would be unable to send adequate reinforcements to Montcalm in Canada and to the French generals in India, and, in the Seven Years' War that began in 1756, Frederick in effect pulled the chestnuts out of the fire for England. Large sums of money, to prove an admirable investment, were sent to Prussia, but the small English forces on the Continent did not cover themselves with glory. Only one general had any very striking success. He was the Marquis of Granby, whose achievements were immortalised on the sign-boards of many English public houses, including that kept by the elder Mr. Weller in the town of Dorking.

Saxony, not directly interested in one of the most wanton of wars, suffered more severely than any of the combatants. Frederick occupied Dresden in 1756, and the Saxon army was compelled to fight against, instead of for, Austria. When the Saxon soldiers protested that such change of fealty was unexampled, Frederick declared that he had no fear of being original. The Prussian King earned the greatest military glory of his reign by defeating the French at Rosbach in Saxony, and the Pompadour, in half fearful admiration, named him the "Attila of the North." But in 1760, Pitt grew weary of the alliance. His object had been attained. Montcalm was dead. Canada was British, and British predominance had been established in India. It was not worth while wasting any more money on the Prussian King.

But fortune never deserted Frederick. He could no longer count on England, but his enemy, Elizabeth of Russia, died in 1762, and Catherine, a German princess, became the virtual ruler of Russia. Frederick's friendship was necessary to her and she withdrew from the war, leaving Prussia in a far stronger position to negotiate with Austria. Peace was signed between England and France in the November, and between Austria and Prussia in the following February. England had gained many things. No other country had gained anything. The position of the French monarchy was imperilled by a long and costly war. As for Austria and Prussia, all conquests were restored, with a return to the *status quo*. Vast treasure had been expended, thousands of men had been killed, towns and villages had been destroyed. And all for nothing.

But while Frederick had not succeeded in annexing Saxony, which was his object at the beginning, he had gained an extraordinary reputation and had established Prussia as one of the great European powers, and—such are the delusions of politicians —the unbelieving coward was acclaimed in England as a Protestant hero. He had waged war with the utmost savagery, and in his treatment of unarmed civilians and undefended cities he had adopted the ruthless policy which has now become the accepted fashion with the introduction of the aeroplane as a weapon of war. Opposed to generals fearful of battle, he adopted the policy of attack with a complete indifference to the loss that attack entailed, and if as a military commander he always lacked courage, he had certainly far more intelligence than any of the leaders who were pitted against him.

The war had left Frederick's hunger for new territory unsatisfied, but his dream of a great kingdom was by no means abandoned. On the very day that he signed the treaty with Austria, he wrote to the Empress Catherine suggesting interference in the internal politics of Poland, and he began the intrigue which concluded nine years later with the first partition of that unhappy country. Poland in the eighteenth century had a coast line on the Baltic and extended southeast to the borders of Turkey. Its government was an aristocratic republic with an elected king. The country was almost entirely agricultural, and the people were fervent in the Catholic faith. The dominant aristocracy had inherited a great tradition of courage and chivalry, but the system of government made progress and intelligent foreign policy impossible. The King could do nothing without the Diet, and any single member of the Diet had the power to veto anything that the King proposed.

Frederick's greed for Polish possessions was not entirely unreasonable, because the Polish province stretching to the Bay of Dantzic cut him off from his own province of East Prussia and was as provocative as the Dantzic corridor, insanely created in 1919 by the Paris Peace Conference. To attain his ambition, he was as anxious for friendship with Russia, "that terrible power which in half a century will make all Europe tremble," as the Empress Catherine was anxious for friendship with Prussia, and it appeared to him that the surest basis on which that friendship could be erected was a treaty by which Russia could grab part of Poland while he grabbed the provinces particularly necessary for Prussian development.

The peculiar character of the Polish government, with the consequent jealousy of the nobles, had led to the frequent election of foreign princes to fill the Polish throne. Henry of Valois, the second son of Catherine de' Medici was King of Poland at the end of the sixteenth century. Three Swedish kings ruled Poland during the next hundred years, and then for another hundred years the throne was occupied by Saxons who rarely, if ever, visited the country. Augustus, Elector of Saxony and King of Poland, died in 1763, and, by agreement between Frederick and Catherine, the nobles were compelled to select a Pole as his successor—Stanislaus Poniatowski, a weak, pliant fool, with whose qualities Catherine was entirely familiar, as he had been one of her many lovers. Unfortunately for Frederick, however, she still had sufficient regard for Stanislaus to protect him from some of the Prussian's predatory plans. He at once began to plot with the Turks in order to terrify Catherine, who, although she denounced him as a disloyal scoundrel, was fearful of his ruthless diplomacy and agreed to his plan of hammering Poland into the surrender of most of her sovereign rights.

War broke out between Russia and Turkey in 1768, and in Paris and London there was no sort of doubt that it had been engineered by Frederick to hasten the partition on which he was resolved. In order that the partition might become practical politics, it was necessary to obtain the acquiescence of Austria, and Maria Theresa declared herself "against all idea of dismemberment of Poland whether in the present or the future." Her son, however, who was now the Emperor Joseph, was more pliable. He had a secret meeting with Frederick in 1769, and the Prussian King took good care that news of this meeting should reach St. Petersburg, in order that the Empress Catherine should be led to fear that, unless she agreed to the partition, it would take place without any territory for Russia.

Meanwhile civil war was waging in Poland, and an outbreak of plague gave Frederick the excuse to send troops into Polish territory to form a sanitary cordon against infection. Prussian troops being sent over the border, Austrian troops promptly followed. The treaty of partition with Russia as one of the three parties was signed at St. Petersburg in 1772. Maria Theresa hated the treachery into which she was forced. "From the commencement of my unfortunate reign," she wrote, "we endeavoured to exhibit at all times a line of conduct true and equitable and of good faith, of moderation, of fidelity to our engagements. They obtained for us the confidence, I may even say the admiration, of Europe, the respect and veneration of our enemies. For a year now all that has been lost. I admit I can hardly bear it. Nothing in the world has hurt me more than the loss of our good name." Frederick had no good name to lose. Maria Theresa was outwitted, but she insisted that, if the partition must take place, Austria must have her full share. "She weeps," said Frederick, "but she takes."

By bribery and force, the Polish Diet was compelled to agree to the destruction of the nation. The 1772 partition was followed by the further partitions in 1793 and 1795. For more than a century,

Poland ceased to exist. For a while it seemed that Napoleon would re-create her, but he was offended equally by her Liberalism and her Catholicism, and it was not till 1919 that an independent Poland once more came into being.

The partition was the work of Frederick, and of Frederick alone. To Catherine it seemed bad politics. She believed that it would have been far more to Russia's interest to be closely allied with an undivided and independent kingdom. To Maria Theresa the partition was immoral. But both women were compelled to agree.

Frederick's greed was not yet satisfied. He was still hungry for Saxony and for the lordship of the whole of central Germany. He was indeed dreaming of that Hohenzollern empire which was to be created by the genius of Bismarck, and to endure for less than fifty years. In July 1777 he embarked on the last of his military adventures with the invasion of Bohemia, but the Prussian forces were obliged to retire owing to disease and desertion. The barbarities in the occupied territory were thorough and characteristic. Everything that could be stolen was stolen, including the roofs of the houses, the windows, and the doors. Wells were poisoned, and attempts were made to introduce infectious diseases into the Austrian camp. Frederick was a thorough believer in frightfulness.

Maria Theresa died in 1780. She was a woman bold and honest and steadfast, a tragic figure of history. Her reign was one long series of troubles —and she was the mother of Marie Antoinette.

The futile Bohemian expedition was the last achievement of Frederick's reign. He was taken ill in 1785, struggled on for a year, and died on August 17th, 1786, at the age of seventy-four. Mirabeau, who was in Berlin at the time of his death, said in a letter to Paris: "There is gloom everywhere, but no sorrow. There is preoccupation, but no affliction. Not a face that does not express relief and hope. Not a sigh, not a word of praise."

CASANOVA

CASANOVA DE SEINGALT
1725–1803

CASANOVA

GIACOMO CASANOVA has his small place in history as an adventurer who, without birth or fortune, and dowered only with enterprise and impudence, succeeded in interviewing kings, hobnobbing with statesmen, and even in amusing the Pope. His eminence in rascaldom is largely due to his birth in the eighteenth century. In an age less frivolous, less sceptical, and less credulous, he would have been merely an ingenious criminal, and his career would have probably been sordid and dull.

His father, Gaetano Casanova, was a second-rate actor, compelled to the stage by a love-affair with an actress, a man of some small learning and an amateur's interest in mechanics. In 1723, while playing in Venice, the susceptible Gaetano fell in love with Zanetta Farusi, the pretty daughter of a leather seller, and, despite the opposition of the leather seller, married her. Giacomo was born in 1725, and, a year later, Zanetta, probably owing to her husband's meagre earnings, herself went on the stage, making her first appearance in London. Zanetta had talent and energy and neither scruples nor morals. Gaetano died when Giacomo was eight, and his mother was continually in engagements, travelling half over Europe, and, at last, after a season in St. Petersburg, obtaining a life engagement in the royal theatre in Dresden. With no father and with a mother entirely uninterested in him, Casanova was brought up by his grandmother, the leather seller's widow, a shrewd, kindly, pious old woman, who cared for him with affection, and to whom he always referred in after years with proper gratitude. Thanks to the bounty of a Venetian poet, distinguished among his fellows for the lewdness of his verse, Giacomo was sent to school at Padua, where he was well taught by a talented master, and he went to the law school in Padua University. M. Joseph Le Gras, Casanova's half-admiring biographer, says:

Mixing in a hodge-podge where others might have been quite lost, Boccaccio and Ariosto with geometry,

Petrarch with dogmatism, Martial, Plautus, and Terence with theoretical and experimental physics, light verses with those of an opposite kind, mathematics with history, the law at which he worked as a student with the magic which he studied secretly. At eighteen he knew Horace by heart and declared he could not live in a country that had no good library. He had a very adaptable mind, and a very prodigious memory. His literary, philosophic, and scientific equipment was much superior to that of his contemporaries. . . . He was always a little superficial. Under a brilliant wit he preserved a bookish mind. His opinions and even his paradoxes were not truly original.

Returning to Venice, Casanova took minor orders, the common resort of the penniless scholar, and set himself to make friends that were likely to be useful, particularly cultivating elderly roués. Venice in the days of its greatness was a city of artists and proud and powerful merchant princes. Venice in the eighteenth century had become "the great pleasure city of Europe," the home of folly and frivolity. Casanova was entirely suited by nature for the dissolute life of the city, but he still had some worthy ambition, and he

[235]

obtained a doctor's degree from Padua with a treatise on law.

Difficulties soon arose. His grandmother died. He lost the most profitable of his patrons through making love to the old gentleman's mistress. And Casanova, always quick in meeting an emergency, sold up his father's furniture and started for Rome. This was the beginning of his life of adventure, and it began badly. He gambled away all his belongings, and was stranded penniless on the road, but, unperturbed and undiscouraged, he cheated his way, first to Rome and then to Naples, making the last part of the journey in considerable comfort thanks to a large sum that he had cozened from a Greek. Casanova was certainly no ordinary adventurer.

The object of his long journey was to visit the Bishop of Martirano, in Calabria, to whom he had been recommended by his mother. But, when he found the bishop living in poverty in a mean house, he packed up his traps and went back to Naples and Rome, to spend what was left of the money obtained from the Greek. At Rome he hoped to obtain employment at the papal Court, and he was presented to Pope Benedict XIV, and, so it is said, made that genial pontiff laugh. But Casanova never understood discretion. His misconduct became notorious, and he was expelled from the Eternal City. From Rome he went to Constantinople, where he was bored, and from there he returned to Venice. The abbé was weary of even nominal loyalty to the Church. The doctor of laws had no taste for law. And, attracted by the uniform and the traditional swagger, Casanova determined to be a soldier. He bought a commission as ensign in the Venetian army, but, as promotion did not come quickly enough, he sold out, and, for want of a better way of earning a living, he was glad enough to secure an engagement to play the violin in a theatre orchestra.

Casanova was never either out of luck or in luck for very long. He was able to be of some small service, which he ingeniously exaggerated, to the wealthy Zuan Bragadin, and secured a friend who remained faithful to him until his death. Bragadin and his friends, in common with a great part of fashionable Venice, having lost their religious belief, were the slaves of superstition. They had exchanged the faith for the mumbo-jumbo of black magic, and, like Cagliostro, Casanova realised that there was a comfortable amount of money for the sorcerer. There is not a shred of evidence to show that he had any real clairvoyant power. That was not necessary—it is not necessary now —for the dealer in mystical spells. The rationalist eighteenth century was as easily beguiled by false prophets as the rationalist twentieth century. And Casanova successfully exploited superstition and the unwholesome appetite for the occult, incidentally beginning the connection with Freemasonry which was to be of great service to him in the future. With the funds obtained by fortune-telling and cabbala, Casanova became a professional, unscrupulous, and most successful gambler. "To live and to gamble were both to me the same thing," he confessed. With his pockets well filled with money, with one love-affair following another, with the protection of Bragadin, life in Venice was pleasant indeed. But Casanova longed for another world to conquer. It was said that Paris was the city "where imposture and the trade of charlatans are able to do their best." So he set out on his first journey to the French capital, having created himself the Chevalier de Seingalt to make welcome the more probable. In Paris he learned to speak French, and he acquired invaluable experience. His self-assurance, never small, grew greater, and he went back to Venice more than ever convinced that the world was his to conquer.

He was home again in 1753, and in the summer of 1755 he was imprisoned in the fearful prison of the Piombi, in a stinking, rat-infested cell. He had over-reached himself. He had aroused the suspicion of the authorities by his intimacy with foreign ambassadors, and particularly with the Frenchman, de Bernis. He had boasted too loudly of his love-affairs, and he had been foolish enough to make a deadly enemy of one of the State Inquisitors. His arrest followed a long and detailed indictment in which, among other things, he was accused of being "an Epicurean and a voluptuary" and "an atheist who pierces the walls of religion and openly mocks all those who practise it."

He remained in the Piombi for nearly eighteen months. Then he managed to escape, probably owing to the bribing of his gaolers by Bragadin, though his own story might have been written by Dumas. And, with money supplied by the same never-failing friend, he again set out for Paris and the beginning of his international career.

Casanova arrived in Paris for the second time on January 5th, 1757, and at once called on the Abbé de Bernis, now Foreign Minister and soon to be Cardinal, with whom he had roystered in Venice. The abbé had no mind that Paris should be told of his Venetian adventures, and Casanova's discretion was purchased with a handsome sum of money and various likely introductions.

Paris in the middle of the eighteenth century was a city of thrill and fascination. "I should regret Paris," said Voltaire, "even if I were sitting at the table of the gods." And foreigners shared the admiration of the native. When the Neapolitan Ambassador was leaving on his appointment as Viceroy of Sicily, the King said to him: "My Lord Ambassador, I must congratulate you on your going to live in one of the most delightful places in Europe." "Ah, sire," was the mournful reply, "the most delightful place in Europe is the one I am leaving, and that is the Place Vendôme."

The nobility had left the old quarter of the Marais—where Hugo was to live years after—for the Faubourg St. Germain. Shops and stalls still encumbered the Pont Neuf when Casanova arrived in the city, though they were removed ten years after. The houses of the well-to-do were new, well designed, and elegantly furnished and decorated. Masked balls were held every week at the Opéra, and, on occasion, there was a royal ball in the theatre of the Tuileries. There were many theatres, the entertainment ranging from opera by Glück to ballet, the drama of Corneille and the comedy of Molière. The boulevards had supplanted the Palais Royal as a fashionable promenade. Longchamp was already popular, and another popular resort was the Coliseum, in the Champs Élysées:

It was a very fashionable meeting-place, an immense circular building erected on one of the large plots in the Champs Élysées (they call it the Circus). In the centre was a lake full of clear water, in which aquatic sports took place, and one could walk around the avenues, which were sanded and provided with seats. At dusk everyone repaired to an immense hall, where a large orchestra played excellent music every evening. Mlle. Lemaure, then at the height of her fame, sang there several times, as did other famous singers. The large flight of steps, which gave access to this concert hall, was the meeting-place for all the gilded youth of Paris, who took their stand under the illuminated doorways, and allowed no woman to pass without making some smart remark about her.

The curse of the city was its mud. Arthur Young, who wrote thirty years after Casanova's arrival in the French capital, says:

The streets are very narrow, and many of them crowded, nine tenths dirty, and all without foot-pavements. Walking, which in London is so pleasant and so clean, that ladies do it every day, is here a toil and a fatigue to a man, and an impossibility to a well dressed woman. The coaches are numerous, and, what are much worse, there are an infinity of one-horse cabriolets, which are driven by young men of fashion and their imitators, alike fools, with such rapidity as to be real nuisances, and render the streets exceedingly dangerous, without an incessant caution. I saw a poor child run over and probably killed, and have been myself many times blackened with the mud of the kennels. This beggarly practice, of driving a one-horse booby hutch about the streets of a great capital, flows either from poverty or wretched and despicable economy; nor is it possible to speak of it with too much severity. If young noblemen at London were to drive their chaises in streets without foot-ways, as their brethren do at Paris, they would speedily and justly get very well thrashed, or rolled in the kennel. This circumstance renders Paris an ineligible residence for persons, particularly families that cannot afford to keep a coach; a convenience which is as dear as at London. The *fiacres*, hackney-coaches, are much worse than at that city; and chairs there are none, for they would be driven down in the streets. To this circumstance also is owing, that all persons of small or moderate fortune, are forced to dress in black, with black stockings; the dusky hue of this in company is not so disagreeable a circumstance as being too great a distinction; too clear a line drawn in company between a man that has a good fortune, and another that has not. With the pride, arrogance, and ill temper of English wealth this could not be borne; but the prevailing good humour of the French eases all such untoward circumstances.

But mud was a small annoyance in the atmosphere of pleasure and easy good humour. "The

Paris of Louis XV," says M. Louis Ducros, "offered the foreigner theatres, promenades, luxury, and all the amenities of life, and those who appreciated such things could enjoy there all the delights of cultivated society once they had been admitted to those famous salons of the eighteenth century." The city was a Mecca to a luxury-loving adventurer, and Casanova's heart must have been gay and his step light when he left the hotel of M. de Bernis with his pockets stuffed with louis d'or and introductions.

De Bernis owed his appointment to the patronage of La Pompadour and the fact that he supported her fatal policy of alliance with Austria against England. But after his appointment, he had the hardihood to protest against the wild expenditure of the Court, and the all-powerful favourite secured his dismissal and exile from Paris. He left the Foreign Office with a cardinal's hat as compensation, but he remained out of favour until La Pompadour's death. Money, money, and yet money, was the cry of the Government and the Court of Louis the Well-Beloved—money for wars, money for the extravagances of Versailles, money for the greedy mistresses of the King. When Casanova came to Paris, money was needed in particular for the military school that had just been built on the left bank of the Seine. Thanks to his patrons and his native impudence, he was appointed one of the agents for a loan, with six offices in different parts of Paris, a commission of six per cent., and a salary of 4,000 crowns. It was as if Mr. Jingle, on his arrival at Rochester, should have been appointed chancellor of the diocese by the bishop. He sold five of his offices for two thousand livres each, and, by the energetic and clever peddling of the lottery tickets, he made, it is said, nearly 100,000 francs in all. This was a good start for his Paris career. The needy adventurer, the cardsharper, the *chevalier d'industrie*, had become, in a few months, a man of money and consequence. So highly did the Government regard the Italian that he was sent to Dunkirk to report on the condition of the French fleet—it was a mad world, in which knowledge and experience counted for nothing in securing employment—and again he was successful and well paid.

Shortly before his fall, de Bernis planned a foreign loan at the lowest possible terms, hoping to tempt the greedy investor with large profits if France won the war. Casanova went as the Minister's agent to Holland, and he persuaded the shrewd Dutch merchants to subscribe the large sum of 20,000,000 livres, of which he contrived, in fair commission and by underhand thieving, to acquire enough to make him *riche d'un million*.

He had realised his heart's desire—money to spend, money to waste, money to burn. "I took," he says, "a splendid lodging near the Rue Montorgeuil." He rented a country house just outside the city. He bought houses. He rioted in the familiar manner of the *nouveau riche*. And the million in a few months became only a few thousands, and Casanova turned to his old methods in order to refill his purse. He started a swindling company for stamping material in colours and patterns, and he allied himself with a gang of card-sharps. He always longed for the life of the great gentleman, but, as M. Joseph Le Gras has said, "there was in him an overflow of low instincts, vulgar, coarse, dirty, the need of immediate satisfaction of low pleasure."

His fall in Paris was as rapid as his rise. In the autumn of 1759 the city had grown too hot for him. His swindles had been discovered. His card-sharping was suspected. Husbands and fathers were denouncing his seductions. But—another almost incredible incident—when he fled to Holland he took with him a letter from the Duc de Choiseul, the successor of de Bernis, to the French Ambassador at the Hague.

For the next two years he was constantly on the move. M. Le Gras has traced the cities and towns that he visited—Paris, Cologne, Stuttgart, Zurich, Solure, Berne, Lausanne, Geneva, Annecy, Aix-les-Bains, Grenoble, Avignon, Marseilles, Toulon, Antibes, Villefranche, Nice, Genoa, Florence, Rome, Naples, Rome, Florence, Bologna, Modenci, Parma, Turin, Chambéry, Lyons, Paris, Strasbourg, Augoberevy, Munich, Constance, Bâle, Paris. "In each town he rested," M. Le Gras says, "he played the *grand seigneur*, gambled, and had time to meet the best society and the worst, to play for high stakes and make conquest after conquest." But Casanova was no ordinary international rogue, and his wanderings must have had a definite purpose. It is suggested that in these years he was a confidential agent of continental Freemasonry. I cannot, of course, attempt to trace the alleged connection of the Grand Orient with the events that culminated in 1789. But in 1760 Masonry was certainly rich, powerful, and international. Casanova was admitted to the craft in 1750, and his connection with it was one of the reasons for his imprisonment in the Piombi. He almost certainly posed in Paris as a persecuted Mason, and this may have opened many doors and many hearts, for not only was Masonry patronised by the philosophers, but it was a craze among the fashionable. De Bernis was possibly a Mason. De Choiseul certainly was. Twenty years later Philippe Égalité was Grand Master of the Brotherhood, "to which," says Prince Kropotkin, "all revolutionaries of renown belonged." It is said that the lodges were kept in touch with each other by travelling agents. Louis Blanc says, in his *History of the Revolution*: "Travelling agents circulated from one place to another, as by an electric wire, the secrets found in the Courts, colleges, chanceries, and in the law courts of all kinds. Certain unknown travellers were seen to wait in towns, whose presence, reason, and aim were a problem." Casanova was one of these agents. What was the nature of the reports he carried, or to what end the money that he spent was given to him, can only be guessed. Perhaps it was of an international revolution that men dreamed in Paris, as men are dreaming now in Moscow.

Casanova inevitably abused the trust that had been committed to him. In every city he became notorious. He borrowed and never dreamed of paying back. He was a boaster who could never keep a secret or respect a confidence, and his employers must have wearied of him long before the protracted itinerary came to an end. In June 1763, Casanova arrived in Calais on his way to England. Four months before, the Seven Years' War had come to an end with the Treaty of Paris. In France

the glory of Louis XIV was forgotten in the humiliation of the loss of Canada and India, thanks to
the foreign policy of La Pompadour. For England
many of the gains of the war had been lost by the
manner in which the treaty had been negotiated.
Pitt had been dismissed. George III was ruling with
a Government of incompetent "King's men," and
Casanova was persuaded that he might induce the
English authorities to float a State lottery and to
give him, as an expert, well-paid employment.

He hurried from the south, only staying in Paris
long enough to collect all his money, and he is
said to have landed in England with £12,000 in
his pocket. He had a letter of introduction from
two Venetian nobles to the Earl of Egremont, one
of the Secretaries of State, of whom Horace Walpole says: "He had neither knowledge of business
nor the smallest share of parliamentary abilities."
But the letter was never delivered, and, though
Casanova remained in London for nine months,
neither banker nor statesman would listen to his
impudent financial suggestions. He managed to
scrape acquaintance with the Duke of Bedford and

one or two other considerable personages, and, thanks to the good offices of the French Ambassador—the Venetian representative would have nothing to do with him—he was presented to the King and Queen. In his *Memoirs*, Casanova describes King George as "a round little man with a face as red as his coat and a feather in his hat, who looked exactly like a fat cock."

Casanova found an old acquaintance in London in the notorious Mrs. Cornelys, a cosmopolitan adventuress, who drew all that part of fashionable London not too particular as to the company it kept, to the assemblies at Carlisle House, in Soho Square, which Horace Walpole described as "a fairy palace." Casanova secured a limited and not unnaturally timid intimacy with some of the smart set of the time, but for the most part his friends in London were the usual riff-raff—sharpers, third-rate dancers, and professional harlots. He took an expensive, furnished house in Pall Mall, and in nine months practically all his money had disappeared. "I had dissipated it," he says, "like a fool, or like a wise man, or perhaps a little like both."

[251]

Wisdom is certainly not apparent in Mr. Bleack-ley's story of his London adventures. He was arrested for an alleged threat, brought before Sir John Fielding, brother of the novelist and one of the Bow Street magistrates, and soon afterwards he was concerned with a forged bill of exchange, and hurriedly escaped back to France in March 1764.

The voyage to England was the beginning of Casanova's decline. "I have made a note of the time, September 1763," he wrote, "as one of the curses of my life. Truly it was after that that I felt myself growing old, though I was only thirty-eight." His adventures in London were with the second-rate. He had hardly been permitted to approach the seats of the mighty. All his schemes for fortune-making had failed. For the first time he began to lose confidence in himself.

After leaving England, he made his way to Berlin, where one of his Italian associates in the successful French lottery was endeavouring to persuade Frederick the Great to authorise a similar flotation. Frederick was difficult, and when Casanova obtained a personal interview, through the good graces of Lord Keith, the King treated him with such scornful disdain that he slunk silent from the presence, persuaded that Berlin was no place for a man of his talents.

But there were still lands to be explored and perhaps exploited. From Germany he went to Russia. Catherine II had just got rid of her husband —a more offensive person never sat on a throne —and had begun her long reign. The masterful lady, "as frank and original as any Englishman," was the patron of philosophers and always attracted by audacity. She received Casanova, but there was never a mention of the official position and the assured salary of which he dreamt. With the half-mad Prince Charles of Courland he dabbled again in alchemy, and he had his small successes in both St. Petersburg and Moscow. St. Petersburg seemed to him an unfinished city, where there were too many similar foreign adventurers for his comfort. Moscow was savage. He could not understand the Russian. He felt himself in a new and bewildering world. Poland appeared to offer better prospects, and he went on to Warsaw in 1766, to be received coldly by King Stanislaus, who owed his throne to the fact that he had been one of the lovers of Catherine and who possibly had been advised by his late mistress of the character of the wandering adventurer. Casanova, however, had almost contrived to force his way into reputable society by fighting a duel with a well-known noble when whispers concerning his past became common, and he was once more invited to continue his journeys. "Our wonderful butterfly," says a contemporary letter-writer, "returns suddenly to his state of caterpillar again."

The next eight years were years of misery and disappointment. He was expelled from Vienna by the police, and from Paris by direct order of the King. He was imprisoned in Madrid and Barcelona. He was very ill in Aix. He wandered from one Italian city to another. Even in these days he had not lost his charm. He bore his misfortunes with distinction. At Rome he was described as "full of wit and vivacity although very poor," and M. Le Gras prints a report concerning him sent by the Venetian Minister to the Republic of Ancona to the Council of Ten. He says:

He who was so rebellious at the justice of the August Council comes and goes in every place with a stalwart look, head carried high, and with a good equipage. He is received in many houses. He is a man of about forty or more, tall in stature, good looking, vigorous, very brown in colour, with a lively eye. He wears a short wig of chestnut colour. They say he is proud and disdainful. He talks a great deal, and his conversation is learned and delightful.

He was in dire need of money, and he looked forward to the future "with no employment, no money, with only a doubtful reputation and vain regrets to feed myself on."

In the autumn of 1774 the Inquisitors of Venice, after repeated pleadings, permitted him to return to his native city. But his old friend Bragadin was dead, and for two years he was compelled to exist on the barest pittance. In 1776 his fortunes took a turn for the better. The Inquisitors engaged him as a police spy, first paying him by results and in 1780 giving him a salary. He set up housekeeping in a small house with a little dressmaker who adored him. He had the entrée to the theatres. Old friends discovered him. His reports to his employers have been preserved, and never did devil more severely censure sin. He reported scandalous behaviour in the theatres. He regretted that Rousseau's *La Belle Héloïse* was sold in the Venetian bookshops. But he hated the obscurity of his employment, and he was probably entirely inefficient, for after a year his regular income came to an end.

Casanova was furiously indignant, and even the memory of past misery could not save him from a wild attack on an influential ecclesiastic who, he believed, was responsible for his latest misfortune, and yet again he was ordered to leave the city. "I am fifty-eight," he complained; "I cannot travel on foot, and winter comes on apace." For some months he wandered over Germany and Holland, and in the autumn of 1783 he was permitted to enter Paris, the city that he loved. "Paris," says M. Le Gras, "made Casanova happy, it made him drunk. It was the most delightful town, full of enchanting chances where dreams easily came true." Casanova dreamt many dreams in Paris in

1783. But none of them came true. He had plans for starting a newspaper—all adventurers sooner or later have such plans—and for cutting a canal from Narbonne to Bayonne. He proposed an expedition to Madagascar, and he was interested in the balloons of the brothers Montgolfier. But he was shabby and old, and no one listened to him. For two months he was persistently importunate. And then another visit from the police, and another order to move on. Casanova had become the cosmopolitan "poor Jo."

In Vienna, however, he was appointed secretary to the Venetian Ambassador, another bewildering preferment for a card-sharp and fortune-telling charlatan, and for a few months he was once more in the great world, dancing and eating with a zest, and actually proposing to marry a well-born young girl. The death of the Ambassador brought the St. Martin's summer to an end, but soon afterwards the Count de Waldstein, an eccentric and wild young man, who was to be concerned in many plots for saving the lives of Louis XVI and Marie Antoinette, offered Casanova the position of librarian in the castle of Dux, in Bohemia. Freemasonry may have been the bond between the two men. Casanova was only too glad to accept, and in a library in a castle, in to him an unknown country, the wanderer spent the last days of his life, violently quarrelling with the servants, writing his most entertaining *Memoirs,* indicting a long remonstrance to Robespierre on the excesses of the Terror. When Waldstein was at Dux the days were pleasant. And when he grew weary of his *Memoirs,* he set down on paper philosophic reflections, not without their shrewdness. He had once visited Voltaire, and he saw himself at Dux another Voltaire at Ferney. He died on June 4th, 1798.

Casanova possessed all the qualities necessary for the adventurer's career. He was good-looking, amusing, rarely easily offended, charming, and genuinely good-natured. Though his trade was swindling, he was often swindled. He had a certain culture, and was not without intellectual interests. He had a talent for making friends, and no man of his character and with his record ever found so many responsible patrons. He failed in rascality because he had no self-restraint. His tastes were low, and what he wanted he must always have at once. So over and over again he destroyed in the folly of a night all that he had created by the ingenious plottings of a year. Still he contrived to die in comfort in the castle of Dux!

TALLEYRAND

CHARLES MAURICE DE TALLEYRAND-PÉRIGORD
1754–1838

TALLEYRAND

IT happens to me almost every day to walk across Hanover Square, and almost every day the Square brings to my mind first George I—in whose honour the Square was named soon after he arrived in England from Hanover with his two grotesque mistresses, one the Maypole and the other the Elephant—and then Charles Maurice de Talleyrand-Perigord, sometimes Bishop of Autun, and afterwards Prince of Benevento, who, in 1830 sent in his old age to England as Ambassador of Louis Philippe, lived on the first floor of the house that then stood at the corner of Hanover Square and Brook Street. Madame de Staël, who knew him well, declared that Talleyrand was the most impenetrable and inexplicable of men. Saint-Beuve believed that no man could adequately write his life. Carlyle referred to him as the "irreverent reverend," and summarised him acutely and, for Carlyle, with quite unusual fairness: "A man living in falsehood and on falsehood; yet not what you can call a false man."

Talleyrand was born in Paris in 1754. Both his father and mother were attached to the Court and knew nothing of home life, and, soon after his birth, Charles Maurice was sent out to nurse. In his third year, possibly neglected by his foster-mother, he fell off a chest of drawers and permanently injured his foot, and the limp that he had all through his life debarred him from the military career that was traditional in his family. If Talleyrand had not limped, he would never have been a priest. If he had not been a priest, he would probably have been among the early *émigrés* and would not have been Napoleon's Foreign Minister. The limp, with its clerical consequence, sent him first of all to the College d'Harcourt, now the Lycée Saint-Louis, in the Boulevard Saint-Michel. The college was one of the best schools of eighteenth-century France, but the training was partial and unintelligent, and Talleyrand's four years there were the beginning of his constant interest in educational reform.

His apologists, remembering the incidents of his later life, would have it that Talleyrand always rebelled against the clerical life. Certainly he took its responsibilities very lightly, but not more lightly than the majority of eighteenth-century English clergymen. There were many and grievous scandals in the pre-revolution Church in France, but to attribute them to its Catholicity and to its allegiance to the Pope is evidence of prejudice and of ridiculous ignorance of the general conditions of the century.

It is quite possible that Talleyrand found his three years in the famous seminary of Saint-Sulpice, where he went after leaving school, tiresome and sometimes irritating, but the discipline seems to have been very light, and the library was comprehensive. It was probably at Saint-Sulpice that Talleyrand first read Voltaire, who was to influence him so vitally, and it was at Saint-Sulpice that he had his first amatory adventures. He was a pale silent boy with grey eyes and bushy eyebrows, a pointed nose and a protruding lip. His hair was long and wavy and his characteristic smile was half cynical and half kindly.

While he was at Saint-Sulpice he spent his holidays at Rheims with his uncle, the Archbishop, a prelate whose piety and devotion were universally recognised. It is of some interest, since the naughtiness of eighteenth-century France has been so grossly exaggerated, that the Archbishop's piety and devotion were not regarded as in any way eccentric. In his uncle's library Charles Maurice read the lives of Richelieu and Retz, and learned the possibility of a prelate playing a great part in the world of material affairs.

Towards the end of his seminary years, Talleyrand went with his father and mother to the coronation of Louis XVI at Rheims. "Never," he wrote afterwards, "did so brilliant a spring presage so stormy an autumn, so dire a winter." Talleyrand saw the coronation of Louis in Rheims Cathedral, and, a few months afterwards, Robespierre, then a schoolboy in Paris, read a Latin address of congratulation to the young King.

Thanks to his uncle, Talleyrand was appointed

[266]

chaplain of the Lady Chapel in the parish church of Rheims while he was still a sub-deacon, and almost immediately afterwards, he was chosen as a delegate to the General Assembly of the clergy in Paris. In September 1775, when he was just twenty-one, he became Abbé of St. Denis at Rheims, with an income of eighteen thousand livres, and with this income he took up his residence at the Sorbonne, where he stayed for two years, reading philosophy and theology. His life was very pleasant in these years when the Revolution was still afar off. Two things must be remembered of Talleyrand if his career is to be understood. The first is that he was an aristocrat to whom bad manners and want of breeding were far more unforgivable than vice and crime, and second that he was as completely the disciple of Voltaire as Robespierre was of Rousseau. He was a laughing unbeliever, at once tolerant and contemptuous. It was a dire misfortune that a complete Voltarian should have been a minister of the Catholic Church, but it is only fair to remember that Talleyrand was only one of the many Voltarian clerics in the

Paris of his day. His birth and his income opened
all doors for him in a society which had escaped
from the sensuous vulgarity of Louis XV and Du
Barry to the pleasanter light-hearted frivolity
created by Marie Antoinette, despite the lumpy
protests of her dour husband. It was a society of
wild extravagance, heavy gambling, strange super-
stitions that made Cagliostro an idol, and grotesque
Anglomania. From his study and his books the
young Abbé would go almost daily to call on
Madame de Genlis in her pleasantly worldly retreat in the Rue Saint-Dominique, and his intimates
included the Comte d'Artois, afterwards Charles
X, Lauzun, who probably lied when he boasted
that he was the lover of Marie Antoinette, Mirabeau, de Chartres, afterwards d'Orléans and Égalité, Gouverneur Morris, that strange American so
intimately concerned with pre-revolution France,
and an intriguing company of philosophers, pe-
dants, aristocrats, and adventurers. It was notorious
that Madame de Flahaut was his mistress and that
she had borne him a child.

In this society—shallow, pleasure-loving, witty

and inquisitive—Talleyrand was a considerable figure. His bitter wit gave him a distinction, and at a time when intellect, thanks to the philosophers, was regarded as highly as birth, his outstanding qualities were sure of ample recognition. Fashionable Paris gambled, frivolled, and philandered, but it also discussed the theories of Rousseau and the criticisms of Voltaire, and, with men like Mirabeau, Talleyrand must often have considered the coming inevitable political changes and the character that they would take.

He was ordained priest in December 1777, and three years afterwards he was nominated by the clergy of Tours as Agent General, the liaison officer between the secular and ecclesiastical authorities, whose duties demanded considerable diplomatic tact. He was a great success, generally wise and very often courageous in the proposals that he made, and in his opposition to the suggestions of more highly placed ecclesiastics. He naturally expected a bishopric as a reward, but Louis, who was immensely conscientious, knew something of the abbé's life in Paris and refused his approval.

[269]

A year or two later, Marie Antoinette prevented Talleyrand from receiving the Cardinal's hat which the Pope, on the urging of the King of Sweden, had been ready to give him. It was not until November 1788 that Louis became properly assured as to his good life, morals, piety, and other virtuous and commendable qualities, and, amidst the discreet laughter of the Paris salons, Talleyrand became Bishop of Autun.

He was now thirty-four and he had already acquired the political principles to which, with all his changes of allegiance, he remained faithful during his life. He wished to see a French Constitution created on the English model, with a limited monarchy, a Parliament consisting of one chamber elected on a narrow franchise, and an hereditary chamber with very large powers of revision and veto. With this as his political ideal, he regarded a close alliance with England as essential to the well-being of France. Alliance with England was the constant object of Talleyrand's diplomacy from the Revolution until the days when, forty years later, he looked out with tired eyes over Hanover Square from his windows in Brook Street.

Before the Revolution, he realised that the chances of gradual and effective reform were minimised by the character of the King and Queen. The King possessed goodness of heart, but that alone was of small value. As Mr. Belloc insists, Marie Antoinette's extravagance has been much exaggerated, but France believed her to be frivolous and light-hearted, and at a time when the nation was passing through an acute economic crisis, frivolity in the Queen was a menace to the monarchy. All this was in Talleyrand's mind when, in May 1789, he came to Versailles to take his place among the higher clergy at the meeting of the States General.

His ideal government was the limited monarchy, and his opposition to the suggestion that the three States should sit together arose, not from any aristocratic disdain of the plebeian, but because he was anxious that nothing should be done at the beginning of the evolution of the government of France to make exact imitation of the English

[271]

model more difficult. At Versailles, and afterwards in Paris, Talleyrand was closely associated with Mirabeau, with whom he frequently quarrelled—it was difficult not to quarrel with Mirabeau—but with whose political opinions he was in almost entire agreement, and the two liberal aristocrats were among the original members of the Jacobin Club in the Rue Saint-Honoré when Robespierre was still an obscure politician and the name of Danton had hardly been heard.

At the first meetings of the States General, Talleyrand met for the first time that other famous revolutionary cleric, the Abbé Sieyès, who was, during the next few years, to make many constitutions and incidentally his own fortune.

Talleyrand must have grown more and more uncomfortable as the revolutionary impetus increased. He disliked violence and disorder, but he hated stupidity more, and it was the stupidity of the Court that made peaceful political evolution impossible, and violent revolution inevitable. A man almost entirely unaffected by sentiment, trained to a cynical realism, and nearly always influenced by cold common sense, is certain continually to be guilty of gross disloyalty, because loyalty to an idea, to a party, to an individual, is a mystical sentiment, generally outraging cool-headed calculation. The first of the many disloyalties of which Talleyrand is accused is disloyalty to the Church in voting in the Assembly for the State appropriation of ecclesiastical revenues. The defence is the more specious because it is eminently reasonable. The appropriation was certain to occur. The nation's need was insistent, and a partial loss of its material possessions might have the most admirable effect on the Church's spiritual health. Coming from Talleyrand, the argument was entirely dishonest. He was beginning to realise that his own position must be increasingly difficult, and he was convinced that, by adopting a position which appeared to be patriotic and unselfish, he was providing some sort of assurance for the future. His action in this matter earned for him, from his outraged clerical brethren, the unpleasant nickname of the "limping Judas."

During the troubled months of 1789, while the

emigrants were pouring over the frontiers, and the Assembly, bewildered and a little aghast, was trying to find remedies for evils and answers to problems, Talleyrand did useful and inconspicuous work on various committees. He delivered frequent speeches in the Assembly, and he was elected one of its fortnightly presidents in opposition to Sieyès. He made no attempt to save the monasteries, but he opposed the frequent propositions that would have taken from the poorer clergy their entire incomes.

Talleyrand's last public appearance as an ecclesiastic was when he said Mass at the altar of the Fatherland on the Champ de Mars on the first anniversary of the taking of the Bastille. It was an unpleasant day. "A north wind," says Carlyle, "moaning cold moisture began to sing; and there descended a very deluge of rain." It is said that Talleyrand whispered blasphemies to Lafayette as he mounted the altar steps. Blasphemies are probably an exaggeration, irreverent jokes are not improbable. The whole situation must have appeared ridiculous to an aristocratic cleric—three hundred

thousand excited people gathered in an amphi-
theatre built by frantic revolutionary enthusiasts.
Priest, deacon, and sub-deacon were Voltarian ra-
tionalists; the whole ceremony was ridiculous, one
of the droppings into melodrama which revolutions
cannot avoid. The actual last ecclesiastical duty
performed by Talleyrand was the consecration of
two constitutional bishops appointed by the Government. In May 1791 the Vatican suspended Talleyrand from his episcopal functions, and ordered
his excommunication if he did not return to pen-
ance within forty days.

Debarred from membership of the legislative
Assembly by the self-denying ordinance adopted
by the members of the First Assembly on the mo-
tion of Robespierre, Talleyrand became a member
of the Department of Paris, retaining municipal
office for eighteen months. Mirabeau had died a
year before. The extremists grew more and more
insistent and influential. Life in Paris became almost insupportable for a fastidious aristocrat, however genuine his democratic sympathies might have
been, and Talleyrand persuaded the Government

to send him as an envoy to London, where he stren-
uously worked for an understanding if not for an
alliance. Despite Napoleon, despite Pitt, despite
all the complications that followed the Napoleonic
conquests, Talleyrand dreamed always of the *en-
tente* which was not to be formally established for
another hundred years.

He was back in Paris when the Swiss Guards
were killed on August 10th—the detached realist
declared that their unnecessarily provocative atti-
tude had occasioned the tragedy—and he remained
until after the September massacres, returning to
London only to learn that he had been denounced
for plotting with the royal family, and was pro-
scribed. His official position, of course, was lost.
He stayed on for some time in England. "Patience
and sleep," he told Madame de Staël, had become
his motto. But he was as fully mistrusted by the
Royalists as by the Jacobins. Pressure was brought
to bear by them on the English Government, and
early in 1794 Talleyrand was ordered to leave
England within five days. He had contrived to bring
his very valuable library from France; part of it

was sold at Sotheby's for two thousand pounds, and this money enabled him to sail to America. He landed at Philadelphia in very straitened circumstances, and it is said that for a time he tried to make a living by selling nightcaps. Washington refused to see him, but he became on friendly, if not on intimate, terms with the famous Alexander Hamilton, the American Radical, with whom he discussed political theories and argued concerning the various benefits of Protection and Free Trade.

Thermidor and the fall of Robespierre promised the revocation of the proscription and a return to France. In January 1796, Talleyrand landed at Hamburg, then a popular refuge for French emigrants and Irish rebels, and it was probably in Hamburg that he first met Madame Grand, the lady who was afterwards, thanks to Napoleon, to become Madame de Talleyrand and Princess of Benevento. She was a very beautiful woman. Madame de Remusat, who hated her, bears testimony to that. But she had no brains and few morals. Rousseau was happy with an illiterate kitchen maid, and Talleyrand for some years was certainly happy with

Madame Grand. She was born at Tranquebar, a Danish possession in India. Her father was French and her mother was a native Indian. When she was fifteen, she was married to one George Francis Grand, a young man born in Wandsworth, whom she left for the notorious Sir Philip Francis, the reputed author of *The Letters of Junius*. She was in Paris some years before the Revolution, living with one wealthy lover after another, and it was this experienced woman, well over thirty, to whose charms the cynical Talleyrand succumbed. As he afterwards explained, a woman of intelligence often compromises her husband. Without intelligence, she can only compromise herself.

From Hamburg, Talleyrand went to Amsterdam and Brussels, and eventually, in the September of 1796, to the Paris of the Directoire, the Paris of vulgar profiteers and venal politicians and more than half-naked women. When Chateaubriand returned to Paris, he said it was like returning to hell. And the Paris of 1796, as immoral as the Paris of 1780, and without its delicacy and refinement, must have been anything but attractive to

Talleyrand. Worse than all, he had to earn a living. Through Madame de Staël, he obtained an introduction to the Directoire, and by the grace of Barras and in opposition to Carnot, he was appointed Foreign Minister. But under the Directoire he was never much more than a clerk, and he only contrived to retain his position by "a miracle of intelligence." To an acute politician, a trained professional subservient to self-seeking amateurs, it was clear that the Directoire had no stability and that it must soon give way to a more intelligent government, and Talleyrand was one of the very first people in France who realised that the new and more stable administration would have Napoleon Bonaparte at its head. In a world of mediocrities, it was not difficult to recognise a rising star. After the treaty of Campo Formio, by which Venice was sold to Austria, and which was signed by Napoleon on his own responsibility, and before Talleyrand had met the conqueror, he wrote him a warm letter of congratulation. And he was thus assured a friendly interview when Napoleon returned to Paris.

Meanwhile the humiliations incidental to the office of Foreign Minister to the Directoire had been made tolerable by a considerable accumulation of bribes. Everything had its price in Paris, and the price was generally, though not always, paid without any beating about the bush. When, in 1797, American envoys came to France to compose the differences that had arisen between the two nations, they were plainly told that the necessary preliminaries were a large loan into the Republic, and a personal gift of fifty thousand pounds to the Directors. Talleyrand was no better and no worse than his associates. He had to live. To live to-day he had a share, a comparatively small share, of the fruits of corruption. To ensure a happier to-morrow, he was fulsome in his public references to Napoleon, who then, as always, had an insatiable appetite for the most exaggerated flattery. The two last years of the Directoire, when Napoleon was pursuing a will-o'-wisp glory in Egypt, were years of gloom and apprehension. The fact that the failure of the Egyptian campaign did nothing to mitigate Napoleon's glory is a sufficient proof of the

[280]

ineptitude of the Government in Paris. With Sieyès and Fouché, Talleyrand played his part in the *coup d'état* of the 18th Brumaire which Napoleon himself almost wrecked by his futile speech at Saint-Cloud, and, with the beginning of the Consulate, Talleyrand was again Foreign Minister, this time with real authority, beginning, with Napoleon, a seven years' series of diplomatic success. M. Bernard de Lacombe says:

He was the author of peace with Europe; he reconciled Revolutionary France with the Russia of the Tsars by framing an agreement with Paul I; he prepared the Treaty of Lunéville, and the Treaty of Amiens; he negotiated the Concordat; he organised Italy at the Lyons conference; he was according to Barante's phrase the political "oracle." All the diplomatists of Europe paid court to him. The reporters, pencil in hand, made hasty notes of his opinions, and repeated them to the public. Poets dedicated their verses to him. Beautiful ladies stuffed his little dog, Jonquille, with sweets. Strangers in Paris wrote his witticisms in their notebooks.

There is no reason to doubt the reality of Talleyrand's early admiration of Napoleon, or of his loyalty to him so long as he appeared to be France's man of destiny. Personal rule was necessary. Effective government had to be created somehow or the other. Talleyrand was always eager for peace, and particularly for peace with England, but the position of France in Europe had, as it seemed to him, first to be established by successful war. War was the necessary preliminary to a permanent peace. But when Napoleon got out of hand and grew drunk with the lust of conquest, then, and not till then, Talleyrand began reasonably and properly to regard him as the enemy of France and no longer worthy of the loyalty of a French patriot. I am convinced that this is the explanation of his career, and that it explains his often denounced treachery. Treachery is a dirty business, but few indeed have been the politicians who in any age have succeeded in living and dying with clean hands.

Talleyrand was largely instrumental in arranging the Concordat with Rome. "I like him," confessed Pope Pius VII, a godly and much harassed Pontiff, and the tribute is striking when Talleyrand's record is remembered. In negotiating the

Concordat he steadily fought for relief for the secular priests, but he did not at all appreciate one of the consequences of the Concordat—the new moral atmosphere of the Tuileries—and he was more than resentful when he was peremptorily ordered to marry Madame Grand. It is unnecessary to follow the long negotiations with Rome that preceded his marriage. Talleyrand was eventually laicised, but that did not mean that he could contract a canonical marriage with a divorced woman, and the evidence that he was ever married by a priest is of the flimsiest. That he ever wanted to marry is even more doubtful. In this connection it may be recalled that, when Talleyrand was asked whether Napoleon had really married Josephine, he answered, "Not altogether."

After the declaration of the Empire, Talleyrand had the difficult task of persuading the Pope to come to Paris for the coronation, and his breeding must have been offended by the vulgar humiliations to which Napoleon subjected his guest. With the institution of the imperial Court he was appointed Grand Chamberlain, probably because he had manners, and might check the effervescence of the ennobled marshals.

It was apparently in 1804 that Talleyrand first realised that the days of glory would soon become the days of disaster unless Napoleon abandoned his ambition of subjecting the whole of Europe to his rule. At Erfurt, at one secret meeting after the other, he persuaded Alexander of Russia to refuse Napoleon's terms, and he resigned his office in 1807, protesting to Napoleon that the first and last sentiment of his life would be gratitude and devotion, and receiving in return the position of Vice-Grand Electorship, with a very large income. "That is another vice for Talleyrand," was the whisper in the Paris salons. In his retirement he was charged with the care of the Spanish princes exiled from their country, with the result that Don Carlos became his wife's lover. "Spain," said Napoleon to him, "has been an unlucky country for both of us."

By 1809, so certain was Talleyrand that the end of the Empire was approaching that he made friends with Fouché, whom he hated. The news of the *rapprochement* of the two most capable men in France brought Napoleon hurriedly back from Spain, and Talleyrand was sent for and violently abused. Talleyrand listened in icy silence, and afterwards commented, "What a pity that such a great man had not a better education."

Out of office and out of favour, he did what could be done to persuade Napoleon against the fatal Russian expedition, and, in the dangerous year of 1813, he contrived to provide no evidence of treachery to Napoleon's myriad spies. He was urged to return to the Foreign Office, but he coldly replied that he did not care to bury himself in ruins. He was to have one more interview with the Emperor. It took place in January 1814, and he was abused again in loud and strident tones. "You are a liar, a traitor, a thief. You do not even believe in God." And Talleyrand politely bowed and kept silence.

After Napoleon, Talleyrand must have found Louis XVIII an easy master. He was a good-hearted, rather lazy *bon viveur*, weary of exile, and willing enough, if he had been able, to attempt the creation of a constitutional monarchy. He was something of a Voltarian, he knew Horace by heart, and, a shrewder man than his brother, he never yielded entirely to reaction. When Talleyrand took the oath of fidelity to the new King he said, "This is my thirteenth oath of loyalty, Sire, and I trust it will be my last."

But, though the Bourbons were rude to him, Talleyrand was the one man who really mattered in the Paris of the Restoration. Metternich came in to gossip with him while he was dressing. The Tsar Alexander remained his friend, and chided the restored family for their suspicions. He was on good terms with Castlereagh, though, after a long consultation with the English envoy, he said: "What a prodigious amount these English do not know." If France had sent a stupid man to Vienna, she would have fared as badly as Germany fared at Versailles. Talleyrand compelled the allied powers to treat France as an equal, and not as a criminal, and by the playing of one State against the other, he made a general agreement for the dismemberment of France impossible.

Talleyrand was in Vienna when news came that Napoleon had escaped from Elba, and he remained outside France during the Hundred Days. He resigned his office in 1816. He was bored with the Bourbons, and for fourteen years he lived in retirement, mainly in his country-house writing his Memoirs, and occasionally appearing at Court to annoy the King by insisting on carrying on his duties as Chamberlain, with some biting comment on current affairs whenever the opportunity arose.

Charles X, the stupidest and most obstinate of all the Bourbons, succeeded his brother in 1824. He intended to be a real king and to have nothing to do with any constitutional nonsense. "For me," he declared, "there is no alternative but the throne or the scaffold." "He forgets the post-chaise," said Talleyrand, and six years afterwards Charles had taken the post-chaise and was an exile in England.

Louis Philippe, the Citizen King, asked Talleyrand to return to the Foreign Office, but he preferred to be Ambassador to England, spending the last years of his active life working for the friendship which he had always desired. His life in London was very pleasant. Only Palmerston, then at the beginning of his career, was difficult, sneering at "old Talleyrand," without anticipating the days when he would be generally known as "old Pam." Talleyrand returned home in 1834. In his last days he was reconciled to the Church, and received the ministrations of the saintly Dupanloup. He died on May 17th, 1838, at the age of eighty-four, "the last cedar of Lebanon."

FOUCHÉ

JOSEPH FOUCHÉ
1763–1820

FOUCHÉ

A T the height of his power there were two
men whom Napoleon feared. One was Charles
Maurice de Talleyrand-Perigord, aristocrat of the
aristocrats, the Emperor's Minister of Foreign Affairs. The other was Joseph Fouché, son of a Breton
sea-captain, Minister of Police under half a dozen
régimes, arch-plotter, and with it all something of
a patriot, who died, five years after Waterloo, almost a millionaire and Duc d'Otranto.

During the Revolution, and in the early days
of Napoleon's rule, the ex-bishop and the sea-captain's son were bitter enemies, and, indeed, Talleyrand once urged Napoleon to order Fouché's execution. But in 1809, when the Emperor was in Spain,
the enemies became friends, and when the news
crossed the Pyrenees that they had been seen walking in Paris arm-in-arm, Napoleon hurried back to
his capital, fearing what might happen.

Joseph Fouché was born in 1763. He was too

sickly to follow his father's robust calling, and he was sent to the Oratorians to be trained as a schoolmaster. Chance took him to Arras to teach philosophy and mathematics, and there he met Robespierre. The two young men, both pale, thin, and dry, destined to be so closely associated in the drama of the Revolution, were in all fundamental respects unlike. Robespierre was the man of theories, the bloodless slave of an inhuman ideal. Fouché was a man of action, unique in history for his ability to squirm out of insistent danger and successfully to retreat with bulging pockets from what appeared inescapable disaster.

In 1789, Fouché was appointed the head of the college in his native city of Nantes. In the Breton capital he found his wife, Jeanne Bonne Coignaud, an extremely plain and affectionate spouse, by whom he had a considerable brood of children. In the early days of the Revolution he was conspicuous for his fervour, and he was sent to Paris as a deputy to the National Convention. He was present at the trial of Louis XVI, voting for "death without appeal and without delay," and in the crazy years that followed he was one of the most vehement and violent of the agents of the Terror. It is impossible for any revolutionary movement to attain its end without a period of terrorism. The national existence of France was threatened. In the hope of recovering their throne, the Bourbons had sold their honour to the foreigner. The new France could not hope successfully to face its enemies unless its people were united, and opposition to the revolutionary *régime* was forcibly suppressed. The Terror was, in fact, a temporary institution of martial law. Politically it is defensible. To the patriot it may well have seemed absolutely necessary. But it could only have been carried out by the scoundrel, and the scoundrel was ready and willing for the task.

Fouché was one of the representatives of the Government sent to La Vendée to repress the Revolution of the Chouans, and in the next year he was in Lyons with the infamous Collot d'Herbois, the ex-actor, and Couthon, who was afterwards to die with Robespierre, guillotining, shooting, glutting the Rhone with corpses, proclaiming that the Republic "must emerge to liberty over the bodies of the dead." Of all the spluttering Terrorists, Fouché was the most vehement. He dearly loved a fine-sounding phrase, and the old pupil of the Oratorians, who had been conspicuous for his love of the gentle Pascal, now scribbled over the gates of cemeteries, "Death is an eternal sleep."

In the spring of 1794, Fouché was back in Paris, proud of his bloodthirsty achievements and still mouthing sentimentalities. "The blood of criminals fertilises the soil of liberty and establishes power on sure foundations," is the most famous of his pronouncements. Danton was guillotined a few days after Fouché's return to the capital. The power of Robespierre was supreme, and it says something for Fouché's courage that he dared to criticise the dictator and to sneer at his endeavour to foist on France a religion of his own invention. The Oratorian turned atheist, having abandoned the old God, was unprepared to worship the new god invented by the ex-advocate of Arras. "You bore me with your Supreme Being," he is reported to have said to Robespierre. For this Fouché was expelled from the Jacobin Club by the dictator's orders, and he began to have a most reasonable fear that Danton's fate would be his.

It was a conspiracy of extremists that contrived Robespierre's undoing—of men of blood who had been his creatures and of men whose loose lives had offended his Puritan soul—Barrère, "the Anacreon of the guillotine," Billaud, conspicuous for his beastly cruelty, Couthon, one of the three butchers of Lyons, Tallien, whose wife Robespierre had arrested, Fouché.

The months that followed were among the most anxious of Fouché's troubled life. Robespierre's death was the signal for a far more complete reaction than his enemies had anticipated. The end of the Terror was the beginning of the end of the Revolution. Collot, Billaud, and Barrère were arrested in May 1795, and in August Fouché was denounced by Boissy d'Anglas, and only saved by the amnesty proclaimed in November with the constitution that established the Directoire. Fouché had a genius for making profitable friendships, and he contrived to obtain the favour of Barras, with whom he had been associated in the plot against Robespierre and who was the chief figure of the Directoire.

Paul François Barras, "a man of heat and haste," was a Provençal of noble birth, of many adventures, and of no scruples—exactly the sort of man to whom revolutions always give a conspicuous if generally a temporary prominence. He was tall and handsome, "only the complexion a little yellow," with a presence and an air, and adroit enough to take full advantage of the popular resentment against the drab Puritanism of a Robespierre. Barras was a great and not too fastidious amorist, and Paris, under the Directoire, recovered all the vices of the Paris of Du Barry without its refinement and the pleasant pretences of the frivolous and now guillotined aristocracy. Barras has an important place in the history of France, since he was Napoleon's patron, finding him a wife in one of his mistresses and giving him the command in Italy. It was his lot to "hold the stirrup for the great captain who vaulted lightly into the saddle."

Perhaps for old comradeship's sake, perhaps because he thought him worth buying, Barras made Fouché an army contractor, always a lucrative employment, and in the course of the next two or three years Fouché acquired, more or less dishonestly, a considerable fortune. In 1799 he began his long career as Minister of Police. Two months after his appointment, Napoleon achieved the *coup d'état* of the 18th Brumaire which brought the Directoire to an end and made him First Consul. Fouché had employed these two months to very great advantage for himself and for his office. The Ministry of Police needed money, so the Ministry arranged that brothels and gambling-hells should be opened in various parts of Paris and should pay him a considerable portion of their proceeds. With these funds in hand he commenced a rigorous repression of his old friends the Jacobins, and by the 9th of November he was a man to be reckoned with. Without his aid and the aid of his police, Napoleon, for all the reputation that he had won in Italy and had not lost in Egypt, could hardly have succeeded in establishing his personal power.

First under the Consulate and then under the

Empire, Fouché was Napoleon's master spy, and the strength of his position was that he always knew much more than he reported. He was hated by Napoleon's brothers. He was feared by Napoleon himself. But Josephine was his constant friend, and out of the comfortable pickings of his office he paid her milliner's bills, and so retained her favour. In all the intrigues of Paris, no secret was hidden from Fouché. He was entirely unscrupulous. When it suited his purpose he would permit the innocent to suffer for the guilty, as when Napoleon fastened on to the Jacobins the responsibility for the plot against his life for which the Royalists were guilty. He would betray his friends with the utmost good humour. Rarely has the world known so complete a ruffian.

At the Ministry of Police, he had one enemy, sure of the favour of Napoleon, whom even he could not disgrace, and one trusty lieutenant on whom he could always depend. The enemy was the Prefect of Police, Louis Nicolas Dubois, a genial, dexterous intriguer, "a ransacker of private lives," quite as ruthless as Fouché, but without the finesse of the master villain. The trusty lieutenant was Pierre Marie Desmarets, an unfrocked priest, an ex-Jacobin, a poet, and some time a clerk in the commissariat department. He had first met Fouché in a Paris gambling-house, and the two men were bound together by collaboration in many villainies, the fidelity of the subordinate being increased by his devotion to what M. Thierry has called "the religion of emoluments."

For all his colossal self-assurance and courage, Fouché must have spent many anxious days in the Ministry of Police on the Quai Voltaire. He was never unaware of the spying of Dubois. He knew of the suspicion with which he was regarded by Napoleon. He knew, too, that many of the most influential of the Ministers, headed by Talleyrand, were his bitter enemies. It must have always been with a certain misgiving that he left his office in the evening for his country-house, to dine with the ugly Jeanne Bonne and afterwards to play whist with a little circle of intimates who had begun life, as he had begun it, as monks, and were now among the spies of his Ministry.

In 1802, Fouché suffered a temporary eclipse. Bernadotte was suspected of plotting against the First Consul, and Fouché was suspected of being privy to his plans. Bernadotte is one of the most curious of the Napoleonic figures. He has been wittily described by M. Thierry as "an armed philosopher, a kind of fighting Quaker, the Franklin of armies." During the Revolution he was the sternest of Republicans, mouthing sentiment in the accepted manner, proving himself a typical Gascon. His military abilities were mediocre. He had failed entirely as a diplomat, and such favours as he received from Napoleon, who really despised him, were due to the fact that he was Joseph Bonaparte's brother-in-law. Napoleon himself had fallen in love with Bernadotte's wife when she was Désirée Clary, the daughter of a "large oil man of Marseilles," and before he had met Josephine Beauharnais. It was the lady's fault that the flirtation was no more than a flirtation, but she was none the less jealous, when she had married Bernadotte, of Napoleon's pre-eminent position in France. It was her resentment of his comparative obscurity that stimulated her husband's ambition, that made him face the risk of rather infantile plots, and that finally landed him and his descendants on the throne of Sweden— the only Napoleonic soldier to retain permanent position among European sovereigns. It is most unlikely that Fouché over-estimated Bernadotte. The plot in which he was accused of complicity was not really serious, but it supplied Napoleon with a sufficient and long-desired pretext for the Minister's dismissal. But Napoleon feared even when he discharged, and, as compensation for losing his post, Fouché was made a senator and presented with twelve hundred thousand francs, and, since there was no available successor sufficiently crafty, the Ministry was temporarily abolished. In the notification to the Senate, Napoleon stated: "Fouché as Minister of Police in times of difficulty has, by his talents, his activity, and his attachment to the Government, done all that circumstances required of him. Placed in the bosom of the Senate, if events should again call for a Minister of Police, the Government cannot find one more worthy of its confidence."

[301]

Fouché nominally retired into the privacy of domestic life and quiet whist parties. But with the money at his disposal he retained his army of spies in his own pay, whenever possible obtaining audience with Napoleon to whisper in his ear that more plots were in the air and that the First Consul's life was in imminent danger. And so insistent and persistent was he, that, a few months after Napoleon had become Emperor, Fouché was again Minister of Police.

Bourrienne tells a story of how Fouché impressed Napoleon by his possession of information which his successors had failed to obtain. Early in 1804 he went to Saint-Cloud to warn Napoleon that Pichegru, the revolutionary general, who had never bowed the knee to the Corsican Baal, was in Paris fomenting another plot. Napoleon, glad to be able for once to score off his old Minister, replied that he had certain information that, two days before, Pichegru had dined at Kingston with one of the English Ministers. But Fouché was able to prove that he was right and that Napoleon's information was wrong, and doubtless this incident had something to do with his re-appointment.

Fouché was still out of office when Napoleon made the most criminal of all his blunders, the execution of the Duc d'Enghien, though he had warned Napoleon of the conspiracy. This example of Corsican vengeance, for which Napoleon himself was alone responsible, and which, followed immediately by the suicide of Pichegru, all the world regarded as a cold-blooded murder, for a time affected Napoleon's position in Europe and antagonised most of the Royalists who had been attracted by the glamour of the Napoleonic successes. Among them was Chateaubriand, who had agreed to become the envoy of France to the Republic of Valais, and who handed in his resignation immediately he heard of the Duc d'Enghien's death. Fouché said of the murder, "It is worse than a crime; it is a blunder." The police spy had retained the tendency to epigram that had characterised the old Jacobin. It suited his purpose at this time to exaggerate the danger of Royalist plots, but about them he certainly had no illusions. "Austerlitz,"

he said at a later date, "has shattered the old aristocracy; the Boulevard Saint-Germain no longer
conspires." The power to conspire successfully had
been lost long before, and, despite the temporary
revulsion caused by the Duc d'Enghien incident,
the Boulevard Saint-Germain was greedily eager to
share the Emperor's favours until his sun began to
set and it was obvious that he had no more favours
to bestow.

Fouché prepared for his return to power by
playing an important, if subsidiary, part in the
comedy that placed on the head of the First Consul
the crown of an emperor. It was he who suggested
in the Senate that a commission should be appointed to report on the advantages of the hereditary rule, urging that the re-establishment of hereditary success was necessary to end the plots
against Napoleon's life, since conspiracies to murder would be useless if one monarch was certain to
succeed another.

When Josephine was crowned Empress in the
Cathedral of Notre-Dame her position as Napoleon's consort was doomed. It was obvious that she

would bear him no child, and it was imperative
that he should have an heir. The divorce did not
take place for another five years, but it was certainly in Napoleon's mind when he crowned himself in Notre-Dame. Negotiations with one royal
family and another took place intermittently before
the alliance with Marie Louise of Austria was
finally arranged, and, at the same time, Josephine
was schooled to accept her fate. In this latter task
Fouché, who had always been her friend, was employed by Napoleon, and it was he who ridiculed
the unlucky woman's suggestion that she should
adopt a baby and pretend that it was her own.

The first four years of the Empire were the years
of Napoleon's greatest glory, the years of Austerlitz and Jena, of the establishment of dominance in
Europe. Fouché remained in his office on the Quai
Voltaire, spying and plotting and contriving to
retain the Emperor's favour. He had his place in
the very mixed society of the Tuileries in the days
when Josephine was Empress, when stable boys had
become courtiers and scarred marshals were chided
for their lack of manners. But Fouché was as con-

vinced as Talleyrand that without peace the Empire could not endure and that the obstinate determination to continue the career of conquest must end in disaster. Both these acute observers scented danger in the Spanish expedition of 1808, and this common apprehension temporarily reconciled the two men who had been enemies for years. Metternich spoke of them as "passengers who see the helm in the hands of a reckless pilot steering straight for the reefs, and are ready to seize the tiller as soon as the first shock knocks down the helmsman."

I have already related how news of a menacing hobnobbing brought Napoleon hurriedly back from Spain. Nothing could be proved against the Minister of Police, and the Emperor sought to assure the continuance of his loyalty by permitting him to join the new nobility with the title of the Duc d'Otranto—a distinction, indeed, for the epigrammatic ex-Jacobin. In the next year Napoleon was in Austria and France was threatened by the futile Walcheren expedition. Fouché acted with great promptness in mobilising the National Guards, for which he was warmly commended by the Emperor.

[306]

But his love of words was his undoing, and Napoleon was furious when he read the grandiloquent manifesto which his Minister had published: "Let us prove to Europe that, although the genius of Napoleon can throw lustre on France, his presence is not necessary to enable us to repulse the enemy."

By the end of 1809 Napoleon himself was at last convinced that peace was necessary, and, perhaps from his love of intrigue, perhaps to force the Emperor's hand, perhaps from a genuine patriotism, Fouché began negotiations with England on his own account. The action was, of course, soon known, and was unforgivable, and in June 1810 he was dismissed from office. He was appointed Governor of Rome, and ordered to proceed there at once, but when he reached Florence he learned that the Emperor had discovered that he had purloined the most important documents in the police archives for use on some future occasion and that the Emperor's displeasure had turned to violent wrath, and Fouché decided that wisdom dictated flight to America.

However, he had a friend and patroness in Elisa,

Napoleon's eldest sister and now Grand Duchess of Tuscany. This was a striking example of his adroitness since he had been notoriously the friend of Josephine, and Elisa, even more than her sisters, hated and envied her brother's wife. Elisa had some of her brother's ability. She was a masterful woman with a capacity for administration. But she posed, she wrote atrocious fiction, and she fancied herself a literary genius, while her blatant immorality earned for her from Talleyrand's bitter tongue the title of "the Semiramis of Lucca." Elisa's friendship with Fouché, begun in 1810, was to prove very costly two years later. Thanks to her intervention, he was permitted to return to France and to live in comparative obscurity and considerable comfort.

If the campaign in Spain in 1808 had appeared perilous, the expedition to Russia was regarded by Fouché as a certain disaster, and at some peril to himself, and, it must be admitted, from entirely patriotic motives, he vainly urged the Emperor to abandon that most disastrous scheme. In the dark days after the return from Moscow, Napoleon, suspicious of everyone and not unreasonably of Fouché, accused him of connivance in plots and then listened to his sage advice. But Fouché knew that the game was up, and he was glad to escape from Paris to Italy, where Murat, King of Naples, was already plotting with the Allies against the man who had made him. He persuaded Elisa to join hands with her brother-in-law, and then, realising that none of the Bonaparte dynasties would be permitted to remain, he managed to be in Paris when Napoleon was compelled to abdicate and the Bourbon Prince, who had fled from France as the Comte de Provence, returned as Louis XVIII.

There were more anxious days for the skilful politician, intimately acquainted with the characters of the men with whom he had to deal, realising to the full the hold that Napoleon, even in defeat, had on the imagination of France, and caring most of all for his own life and his own possessions. He was at the head of the deputation of the Senate that received the King when he made his entry into Paris. He urged him not to forget the Revolution and to consider carefully how the French people, after twenty years, could best be reconciled to the resumption of Bourbon rule, and, to gain the royal favour, he wrote to Napoleon in Elba urging him in the cause of peace to withdraw to America. Louis listened to Fouché but he would not employ him. He knew quite well that he had not returned to pre-revolution France and that new men were needed in the new world, but he had no mind to give office to the butcher of Lyons and La Vendée. It was only when news reached Paris of Napoleon's escape from Elba that the King began to think that it would be wise to have a capable Police Minister in his employ. But it was too late, and Fouché wrote to the King: "The only plan to adopt is to retire."

Shortly before he crossed the Belgian frontier to begin his second exile, this time only of a hundred days, Louis appointed Bourrienne, who had been for years Napoleon's private secretary, Prefect of Police, with insistent instructions to arrest Fouché. But the master policeman had no difficulty in escaping from the amateur. It is said that in the course of his escape, without knowing where he was, he hid in the garden of Queen Hortense, Napoleon's stepdaughter and sister-in-law, and, finding himself among enthusiastic Bonapartists, he determined once more to serve the Emperor. But the truth probably is that Fouché believed that Napoleon had at least a sporting chance of regaining and retaining power, and that consequently it seemed advisable once more to be in his service. Napoleon, once more in Paris after his triumphal progress from the Mediterranean coast, was in no position to pick and choose his Ministers. He certainly would vastly have preferred to have ignored Fouché. But it was pointed out to him that, despite his title of Duc d'Otranto, Fouché was still the one man who could propitiate the Jacobins, and he again received his old portfolio of Minister of Police. And it was Fouché, who in all the chameleon-like changes of his career, never lost his love of the large word, who persuaded Napoleon to insert in his declaration to the French people, "Sovereignty resides in the people. It is the source of power."

Any belief that he may have had of a permanent Napoleonic restoration disappeared long before

[311]

Waterloo, and with a view to the future, and while still taking Napoleon's pay, he was busy corresponding with Metternich in Vienna and with Louis XVIII at Ghent. A story is told of a master stroke of duplicity which may or may not be true. Fouché is said to have sent to the Duke of Wellington a copy of Napoleon's plan of campaign, written in cipher, and to have caused the messenger to be arrested on the Belgian frontier. If Napoleon had succeeded, the treachery would have remained unknown. If Napoleon failed, the existence of the undelivered letter might be regarded as proof of devotion to the cause of the Bourbons.

Perhaps the most bewildering event in Fouché's career is the fact that, after Waterloo, Wellington warmly urged his re-appointment to the Ministry of Police. Bourrienne sarcastically writes: "After all the benefits which foreigners have conferred upon us, Fouché was indeed an acceptable present to France and to the King. . . . In less than twenty-four hours the same man had been entrusted to execute the most opposed and the most contradictory measures. He was one day a Minister of

usurpation and the next day the Minister of legiti-
macy." Bourrienne is never reliable, and, as he was
anxious to be Prefect of Police, and the appointment was impossible with Fouché as Minister, his
irritation is not difficult to understand. He relates
that Paris received the Bourbon King with enthusiasm, and that Fouché, in order that it might not
be supposed that his services were unnecessary,
sent "wretches to mingle with the crowd to sprinkle
destructive acids upon the dresses of the females
and to commit acts of indecency in order to prevent respectable people from visiting the gardens
of the Tuileries through fear of being insulted or
injured."

Fouché, with Coulaincourt and Carnot, the or-
ganiser of victory, who retained his honour and his
soul through all the changes of the Revolution and
the Empire, was appointed one of the Commis-
sioners to treat with the Allies, and he was one of
the five members of the provisional Government
chosen to hand over executive powers when the
King again reached Paris.

Talleyrand became President of the Council

and Secretary for Foreign Affairs in the King's new Ministry. Fouché was Minister of Police, and the other five Ministers were old Royalists. But the services of Fouché were not long retained. Bourrienne claims that he was responsible for the dismissal. He relates that, in an interview in the Ministry, Fouché expressed his opinion of the Bourbons with great freedom and disrespect, that he at once reported the conversation to the King, and that Fouché's disgrace was the result. "I had the satisfaction," he wrote, "of having contributed to repair one of the evils inflicted upon France by the Duke of Wellington." Better men than Bourrienne had marvelled at Fouché's appointment. Chateaubriand saw Talleyrand and Fouche going out together from the royal audience chamber, and he bitterly remarked: "See vice leaning on the arm of crime." Fouché attributed his fall to Talleyrand. Crime felt that it had been betrayed by vice. "You are dismissing me, you scoundrel," he said to the President of the Council. "Yes, you imbecile," was Talleyrand's reply. Talleyrand was an aristocrat, and much might be forgiven him by the Bourbons.

Fouché's record was too notorious for a Bourbon, now that Napoleon's career had obviously come to an end, to forgive. He was sent as Ambassador to Saxony, but in 1816 he was tried in his absence for participation in the execution of Louis XVI, and condemned to death. Fouché was undisturbed by this childish vengeance. He had retained the immense fortune accumulated at the Ministry of Police. He made his home in Trieste, became a nationalised Austrian, and died a millionaire in 1820.

Fouché was no coward, and certainly no toady. Ready as he was for any treachery when it seemed likely to be profitable, he more than once risked everything by refusing to approve a policy which his subtle mind told him was ill-advised. No man during Napoleon's reign was more hated, but he was aloof, indifferent, and domestic. In his early Jacobin days, his cruelty was notorious. In his days of power he was detested as much as he was feared. His retention of office is the tribute to his outstanding ability. He was, indeed, the shrewdest of politicians, with a genius for anticipating events and estimating human qualities. There is no sort of evidence that his conscience was ever troubled by the slaughter of Royalists or the betrayal of friends. The only fear that he ever seems to have experienced was an occasional apprehension that some sort of punishment might follow the crime. But one never knows. He was only fifty-seven when he died. And he looked eighty.

ROBESPIERRE

MAXIMILIEN MARIE ISIDORE ROBESPIERRE
1758–1794

ROBESPIERRE

IN the year 1775, King Louis XVI of France, then barely twenty-one and recently come from his coronation in Rheims Cathedral, made a progress through his city of Paris to the Cathedral of Notre-Dame, and stayed for a while at the college of Louis le Grand, on the borders of the Quartier Latin. The students were drawn up to welcome the young King. Among them was a happy, laughing madcap, Camille Desmoulins, who was to add sweet savour to the horrors of the years to come, but the boy selected by the masters, for his capacity and assiduity, to read the Latin speech of welcome was François Maximilien Joseph Isidore Robespierre, the son of a lawyer of Arras, and then in his seventeenth year. It was a dramatic meeting—the King shy, uncomfortable, self-distrustful, and the boy, destined to be the most formidable of his enemies, with his slanting forehead, his thin lips, his turned-up nose, his short-sighted eyes, and his characteristically precise dress.

Robespierre has become one of the super-villains of popular history. He possessed none of those qualities that provide for the average man some excuse and compensation for the worst sins. He was as drab as Louis XI. He has been clearly summarized in striking phrase by Carlyle, and in his acute study Mr. Belloc has striven to explain him. But no man has tried to excuse him. He is almost the only unwhitewashed of historical bad men. Yet he had his virtues, as even Carlyle admits. He was the victim of his limitations, and there were men who loved him, some of them very worthy men, even in the days of his defeat.

Revolutions are fruitful of villainy, and afford ample opportunities for villains. At certain epochs in history it is necessary to pull down, but political housebreaking is not a profession for the overscrupulous. It is ridiculous for the amiable Liberal, who welcomes the results of revolution, to suppose that they can be attained without a period of ruthless repression and wholesale execution. There

comes a time in the evolution of any new order
when either revolution or counter-revolution must
triumph, and when triumph can only be gained for
either side by the elimination of the opposition. I
am not attempting any defence of the Terror in
Paris of 1793 or of the infinitely more bloodthirsty
Russian terror since 1917. I am merely insisting
that a successful revolution is impossible without a
guillotine or a gallows, a fact which makes me an
anti-revolutionist and which cannot be ignored in
attempting to understand the character, the excesses, and the crimes of famous revolutionists.
There were in revolutionary France—there doubtless are in revolutionary Russia—men who genuinely enjoyed cold-blooded killing; but, in so far
as he was responsible for the Terror, it was to
Robespierre a perfectly hateful political necessity
to which he was impelled by patriotism and a narrow devotion to a political formula. And perhaps
there are Robespierres in Bolshevist Russia.

Robespierre was the eldest of four children. His
mother died when he was seven, and his father,
whose heart was broken by his wife's death, died

three years later. In 1781 Maximilien finished his studies in Paris and returned to Arras, where he began to practise as a lawyer, lodging with a sister and living a hard, frugal, and eminently virtuous life. He was a thorough, industrious young man, with a passion for platitudes and not the smallest sense of humour—as Mr. Belloc insists, a typical member of the French professional class, with exactly those qualities necessary to small professional success in a small French provincial town. So considerable was his reputation that, while he was still in the middle twenties, the Bishop of Arras appointed him judge of the local seignorial court, a position which he resigned rather than condemn a convicted criminal to death. This was a highly characteristic incident, an indication of the true spirit of the man. While he was studying and practising law, Robespierre was busy reading Rousseau. It has been said that the *Contrât Social* was the Bible of the Revolution. It was certainly Robespierre's Bible. He was the complete Rousseauite. From Rousseau he derived his entire political philosophy, and, when power came to his hand, his one en-

deavour was to put Rousseau's theories into practice. What Lenin was to Karl Marx, Robespierre
was to Rousseau, though it appears certain that,
when there is sufficient knowledge to make com-
parison possible, Lenin will appear by far the
greater man.

With many extravagancies, Rousseau laid down
what has generally become the accepted doctrine
of democracy, and it was to Rousseau's theory of
the rights of man that Robespierre was consistently
faithful in all the terrifying experiences of his political life. He accepted from Rousseau the corresponding doctrine of the immortality of the soul.
But he never realised that rights imply duties. He
never learned that men are bundles of complex
inconsistencies, not to be summarised in any formula. He was—I quote Mr. Belloc—"a man of
conviction and emptiness too passionless to change,
too iterant to be an artist, too sincere and tenacious
to enliven folly with dramatic art or to save it by
flashes of its relation to wisdom." There is only
one other man in history, as it seems to me, to
whom Robespierre can accurately be compared, and

that is Calvin, another Frenchman. Both were extreme Puritans, compelled to persecution by the conviction of the wickedness of everyone who differed from them.

In the autumn of 1788, news reached Arras that the States General were to be assembled, and Robespierre offered himself as a candidate, issuing a sententious election address which concluded: "The Supreme Being will hear my prayers. He knows their sincerity and their fervour. I can hope that He will favour them." He was elected, and in May he was present at the first meeting of the States General at Versailles. "The meanest of the six hundred," Carlyle calls him, "an anxious, slight, ineffectual-looking man, under thirty, in spectacles; his eyes (were the glasses off), troubled, careful; with upturned face, snuffing dimly the uncertain future time; complexion of a multiplex atrabiliar colour, the final shade of which may be the pale sea-green."

He made many speeches in the Assembly, apparently very long and very dull. He was a prototype of the House of Commons bore. His voice was weak and his gestures were awkward. And, as all through his life, he was always careful of his dress and appearance, avoiding extravagance, never forgetting proper professional dignity. Although he was ignored by the majority of his colleagues, the greatest of them realised that he was exceptional and that he was sincere. "That young man believes what he says," said Mirabeau. "He will go far." Robespierre on his side, recognising genius and, as a Puritan should, reprobating immorality, commented: "Mirabeau's position will be destroyed by the evil effect of his morals."

He remained a comparatively obscure parliamentarian during the great events of the summer of 1789—the capture of the Bastille, the burning of the houses of great nobles in the countryside, the launching of the Revolution. In the parliamentary debates he was concerned with small details, testing everything by the Rousseau formula, insisting always on legalities. October came with the Mænads at Versailles and the moving of the Assembly to Paris. And in Paris, Robespierre first began to gain an influential political position.

The Jacobin Club had established itself in an old convent in the Rue Saint-Honoré in December 1789, and three months afterwards Robespierre was elected its President. The Jacobins loved talk. Night after night they met to listen, and Robespierre was there to talk. His speeches were immensely long. Louvet, who hated him, jeered at his eternal declamations, his innumerable repetitions, and his absurd contradictions. He revelled in *clichés* and he loved platitudes. But the Jacobins could never have too many speeches from him, and the speeches could never be too long. It was the backing of the Jacobin Club that made Robespierre's career.

In the Assembly he remained faithful to Rousseau, and he voted that Protestants, Jews, and even actors should be given votes. He was opposed to a property franchise. A man must have a vote because he was a man, not because he paid taxes or had a bank balance.

As time went on, and again largely owing to the Jacobin Club, Robespierre came to be regarded as one of the leaders of the Left, and to be counted by the Royalists, with Marat and Danton, as the most venomous of their enemies. No three men could have been more unlike: Robespierre the Puritanic pedant; Danton the magnificent, fearless man of action; Marat, most maligned of them all, tumultuous, unkempt, the one prominent revolutionist who really loved the poor and was loved by them.

Mirabeau died in 1791, and with his death the first stage of the Revolution came to an end. Robespierre was living very quietly in Paris, writing out his speeches, generally alone, sometimes spending an evening with Camille Desmoulins, at whose wedding he was a guest; more rarely at Madame Roland's, listening silently to highfalutin' talk about political changes, and naïvely enquiring, "What is a Republic?"

Louis had mistrusted Mirabeau, but with his death he began to despair. Two months after, there occurred the melodramatic flight to Varennes and the ignominious return to Paris. Robespierre hotly denounced the King's action as treason in a speech at the Jacobin Club, with Lafayette and Bailly, the very moderate Mayor of Paris, among the audience.

Paris was in ferment. There was imminent risk of reaction. The lives of the revolutionary leaders were in considerable peril. On July 14th, six hundred Marseillais, whose march inspired Rouget de Lisle's great hymn, came to Paris, with thousands of other provincials, for the second great federation on the Champ de Mars. Two days afterwards there were riots outside the Tuileries, and whispers everywhere of insurrection, counter-revolution, treachery. Revolutionary printing presses were destroyed. Danton, Desmoulins, and Marat were in hiding. In the early evening the Jacobin Club was hot and crowded with indignant and fearful men, most of whom stole away before the end. Robespierre endeavoured to calm the anxious excitement. When the meeting was over, he was met at the door by one Duplay. a master builder and a man of some fortune, who, fearful for his leader's safety, persuaded him to come back with him to his house near by in the Rue Saint-Florentin. It was midnight when they arrived at what was to be Robespierre's refuge for the rest of his life, where he was welcomed by Duplay's wife and his plain daughters, and where he was to live in an atmosphere of admiring security.

The Duplays gave Robespierre unaffected, unobtrusive affection, and the man to whom this affection was offered by a typical French *bourgeois* family, of all people on earth most acute, was not unworthy of it. Robespierre was passionless, but he was hungry for understanding and adulation. He loved sitting with the admiring Duplays, with his bust in one corner of the room and the walls decorated with his portraits. He was always amiable, always eager to explain the reasons for his actions, never wearying of the quiet domesticity. He spent his evenings with the Duplays in the midst of the worst horrors of the Terror. He was there when Louis XVI was hurried to the guillotine. He sat behind the curtains of his room listening to the rumbling tumbril that carried Danton along the Rue Saint-Honoré to his death.

At the end of 1791, Robespierre went home to Arras for a short holiday, to receive and to enjoy the admiration commonly given to a local hero. The Legislative Assembly, the successor of the Constituent Assembly, met for the first time on October 1st of that year. Thanks to Robespierre, it had been decreed that none of the members of the Constituent Assembly should be eligible for election. The idea was that the ablest of the Royalists would be eliminated. The Assembly was largely dominated by the group of moderate middle-class revolutionists to be known as the Girondists, led by Vergniaud, a lawyer from Bordeaux. Robespierre was, of course, outside the Assembly, but from the Jacobin Club he lectured, criticised, and denounced.

The *émigrés* exiled in Austria and Prussia were persistently intriguing against the Revolution, and were, it was suspected, in constant communication with the King. The Girondists determined that their property should be confiscated and that war should be declared on Austria. The King resisted, but finally was compelled to agree to both propositions, and to appoint a Girondist Ministry, with Roland as Minister of the Interior. Robespierre opposed the war. Louvet says, indeed, that he made fourteen speeches against it in one week, until even the faithful Jacobins were bored to sleep. The revolutionary machine had now been set going, and the pace soon grew hot. The King's bodyguard was disbanded. It was proposed to banish all priests who refused to take the oath to the Constitution. The King, plucking up courage, dismissed the Girondist Ministers. Lafayette was once more in power, and openly attacked the Jacobins. The provincials were back in Paris for July 14th. Patriotism was inflamed by the invasion of French territory by the Duke of Brunswick. And Paris rose. On August 10th the Swiss Guards were massacred —a young artillery officer called Napoleon Bonaparte watching the rioting from a neighbouring window—and the royal family was imprisoned.

Robespierre hated disorder. Men have said that he was a coward. Perhaps he was. Certainly rioting was not his *métier*. He spent August 10th quietly at the Duplays'. Two days afterwards he attended the session of the Paris Insurrectionary Commune. Retiring, neat, respectable as he was, it was to him that the rebels looked as their leader, and he repaid them with another of his very long speeches, to which, it should be added, they listened with exemplary patience. The situation was queer, perplexing, almost inhuman—impossible, perhaps, anywhere but in France. Robespierre concluded with a grandiloquent peroration:

The whole people of France, so long degraded and oppressed, felt that the moment has arrived to fulfil that sacred duty imposed by nature upon all living, and more especially upon all nations—that, namely, of providing for their own safety by a generous resistance to oppression. Thus has commenced the most glorious revolution which has honoured humanity. Let us go further, and say the only one which has had an object worthy of man—that of founding political societies on the immortal principles of equality, of justice, and of reason. What other object could have united, in one moment, this immense people, these innumerable multitudes of citizens of all conditions, making them act in concert without chiefs, without watchwords? What other cause could have inspired that sublime and patient courage and have given birth to miracles of heroism superior to all which history has related of Greece and Rome?

His speech finished, the Commune chose Robespierre as their spokesman to the Assembly, to demand the election of a National Convention and the institution of a revolutionary tribunal. The first result was the return of the Girondists to office, with, this time, Danton as Minister of Justice. But fear still lurked in the streets. A fortnight afterwards, the Prussians captured Longwy, and on September 2nd the Paris mob broke open the prisons and, it is said—the number is probably exaggerated—massacred twelve hundred prisoners. The Convention met on October 1st, and on the next day the monarchy was abolished. The majority of the Convention was Girondist, but the deputies from Paris were Men of the Mountain, and the debates became wrangles between Paris and the provinces. Robespierre was the unchallenged leader of the Mountain. Danton was busy stirring up patriotic fervour and contriving the defeat of the invader. Marat, who was to be assassinated within ten months, had been directly concerned in the September massacres, and was suspected and hated. On October 29th, Robespierre was violently attacked in the Convention by Louvet, "a thin, lank, pale-faced man," in a speech anticipating in its form Zola's famous *J'accuse*:

Robespierre, I accuse thee of having long calumniated the best and purest patriots. I accuse thee because I think the honour of good citizens and of the representatives of the people belongs not to thee.

I accuse thee of having calumniated the same men, with even greater fury, during the first days of September; that is to say, at a time when thy calumnies were proscriptions.

I accuse thee of having, so far as in thee lay, wilfully misunderstood, persecuted, and vilified the representatives of the nation, and of having caused them to be misunderstood, persecuted, and vilified by others.

I accuse thee of having continually thrust thyself forward as an object of idolatry; of having suffered it to be said in thy presence that thou wert the only really virtuous man in France, the only man who could save the country, and of having at least twenty times said as much thyself.

I accuse thee of having tyrannised the Electoral Assembly of Paris by every ruse of intrigue and intimidation.

I accuse thee of aiming openly at the supreme power.

Robespierre was terrified by this outburst, and he demanded a week in which to prepare his defence. The demand was supported by Danton, and the Convention agreed. The carefully written defence is tiresome to read, and, one would suppose, must have been tiresome to hear. It contained the usual *cliches*, the usual classical references, the usual self-satisfaction, and the usual peroration:

I am told [concluded Robespierre] that one innocent person perished among the prisoners, some say more; but one is doubtless too many. Citizens, it is very natural to shed tears over such an accident. I myself have wept bitterly over this fatal mistake. I am even sorry that the other prisoners, though they all deserved death by the law, should have fallen by the irregular justice of the people. But do not let us exhaust our tears on them; let us save a few for ten thousand patriots sacrificed by the tyrants around us; weep for your fellow-citizens, dying beneath the ruins of their homes, shattered by the cannon of those tyrants; let us reserve a few tears for the children of our friends murdered before their eyes, and their babes stabbed in their mothers' arms, by the mercenary barbarians who invade our country.

After the speech there was a violent scene. The gallery wildly applauded, and, despite the protests of Louvet, the Convention passed the order of the

[335]

day. Robespierre had conquered, and he quickly
followed up his success. The Girondists had no
policy. They were moderates at a time when moderation was merely grotesque, and Robespierre, feeling for a policy, and, as he said, and probably
truthfully, abhorring the penalty of death, began
to demand the trial and execution of the King.
While he lived there could be no peace. "Louis
must perish because our country must live." The
logic is bloodless, unanswerable, eminently French.
A dethroned king must be, while he lives, the focus
for anti-revolution, and so on January 19th, 1793,
Louis Capet was brought to his trial. When, late
on the following day, his judges one by one ascended the tribune to vote, and give their reasons
for the vote, Robespierre talked at length. "I know
nothing," he said, "of that humanity which is for
ever sacrificing whole peoples and protecting
tyrants. I vote for death." His turgid rhetoric was
in dramatic contrast to Danton's—"I am not a
politician; I vote for death"—and to the four words
of the Abbé Sieyès, *"La mort sans phrase."*

Louis was executed the morning after his condemnation. The tumbril passed the house of the Duplays, and Robespierre thoughtfully had the doors and windows shut that the daughters might not be disturbed. The execution, defensible as it might be from a revolutionary point of view, appeared to be an immense political blunder. Within a fortnight France was at war with the whole of Europe. Threatened by kings, she had thrown down the head of a king as a gage of battle!

The situation in the early months of 1793 was a tragedy interwoven with a tragedy. The execution of the King, to which the Girondists had consented, strengthened the hand of the extremists. The Convention representing France was terrified by the Commune of Paris. In its debates, the galleries were filled, not only with members of the Jacobin Club, but by genuine rough, rude, and sometimes ragged citizens from the Paris slums, who jeered and interrupted. There was chaos in the capital, while disaster after disaster occurred in the armies, culminating in the treachery of Dumouriez and the not unreasonable fear that Brunswick and his Prussians might be in Paris within a fortnight. With

[337]

the peril came the man. On the Champ de Mars, Danton had already called France to arms with that magnificent and most thrilling of all slogans: *"L'audace, encore l'audace, toujours l'audace."* Now he worked as never man worked before, with his heart broken by the death of his wife, to compel the Republic, only a few weeks old, to save herself. But it was clear to his strong, realistic mind that there could be no victory in the field while there was only talk in the capital. By some means or the other, order must be restored. Parliamentary government, from which the English-loving Liberals had expected so much, had failed, as it nearly always fails in moments of great crisis, and it was Danton who, perhaps a little fearfully and certainly for motives of patriotism and high expediency, was the creator of both the revolutionary tribunal and of the Committee of Public Safety, which came into being in April 1793, and of which he was one of the nine original members.

The story of the Terror begins with the creation of the Committee of Public Safety. It is impossible to understand the Revolution, or the characters either of Danton or Robespierre, if it is not realised that the Terror was a dictatorship without which the Republic would most assuredly have been strangled in its babyhood and the monarchy restored by foreign soldiers. All through these months Danton had striven to save the Girondists and to hold the whole Republican party together. But the Girondists were unpractical idealists, terrified by the situation that they had themselves created, hating and dreading the Paris mob, which they could not control. And with the political complications and the military disasters it became more and more obvious that there was an immense difference in political theory between the Men of the Plain and the Men of the Mountain.

Robespierre was comparatively inconspicuous, while Danton was raging, tearing, and exhorting. But he went on making speeches. In one of them, in a debate in the Convention in February, he demonstrated that his heart still remained with Rousseau. He said:

We should declare that the right of poverty is limited, as all others, by the obligations of respecting the rights

[339]

of the others; that the right of property must not be injurious either to the security or to the liberty, or to the existence, or to the property of other men; and that every trade which violates this principle is essentially illicit and immoral.

He demanded also that the right to work be proclaimed, though in a very modest form:

Society is bound to provide for the subsistence of all its members, either in procuring work for them, or in guaranteeing the means of existence to those who are unable to work.

Having been compelled to accept the revolutionary tribunal, the Girondists made the fatal blunder of attempting to use it. Marat, whom they impeached, described himself to his judges as "the apostle and martyr of liberty," against whom a faction of notorious intriguers had obtained a decree of accusation, and was promptly acquitted, to become even more popular with the Paris mob.

The Commune now threatened the very existence of the Convention, and the Girondists, again blundering, ordered the arrest of Hébert, one of the complete scoundrels of the Revolution, an ex-

[340]

journalist turned pamphleteer, whose infamous publication, *Le Père Duchesne*, had printed scurrilous libels on Madame Roland. "There was something of the pickpocket in Hébert," says Mr. Belloc, "and not of the pickpocket only, he was also a blasphemer, an atheist, a man delighting in the foulest words and in the most cowardly or ferocious of actions." He was arrested, but the Commune, of which he was a prominent member, was too strong for the Convention, and secured his release.

As summer approached, Danton grew weary and ceased to control the Committee of Public Safety, to which Robespierre was now nominated, soon to become its dominant member. A successful insurrection in La Vendée added to the rage of Paris against the Girondists, and thirty-one deputies, with Madame Roland, were put under arrest. The Girondists loved words as much as Robespierre loved them, and were even more their slaves. They burned with "a passionate love of humanity," and, as has been subtly said, "the Revolution devoured them because they failed to interpret her enigmas." Marat was stabbed by Charlotte Corday in July.

Marie Antoinette, Philip Égalité, the royal regicide, and the Girondists were guillotined in October and November. The Terror was in action. Robespierre has been commonly held responsible for all the excesses. As a matter of fact, for a few months almost unlimited power was in the hands of Hébert and his associates. Robespierre dared not oppose, and—I quote Mr. Belloc—"he excused in platitudes." And the Terror had this justification—that, while the guillotine was busy, Carnot was organising victory.

Danton was back at the Convention at the end of November, eager to bring the Terror to an end. At the moment it seemed that France was saved. Such defence as there had been for ruthless dictatorship was no longer possible. Danton was sure of Desmoulins, and he hoped for the support of Robespierre. But Robespierre, the incorruptible, the pedant, the man of theory and of pity, had become drunk with power. He was afraid that, if the machine were destroyed, he, too, would be destroyed. In his refusal to co-operate with Danton he was supported by his two intimates, Saint-Just, that appealing figure of tragedy, and Couthon, the half-paralysed Auvergnat, and probably also by Carnot.

While Robespierre's finicky soul could tolerate massacre, he found blasphemy insufferable. On November 10th the Hébertists arranged the infamous feast of the Goddess of Reason in the Cathedral of Notre-Dame, second-rate actors and prostitutes posturing at the high altar. Robespierre had always been opposed to the anti-religious policy of the Revolution. Like Rousseau, he was a Deist. He loathed and despised Hébert, and he was now convinced that Hébert and the disorder which he represented must be suppressed. Throughout the winter he did nothing. Danton was in Paris, and the man of theory feared the man of action. Desmoulins, in his *Vieux Cordelier,* suggested developments which might be the end of Robespierre as well as of the Terror. The agents of the Committee of Public Safety, back from the provinces with their hands red with blood, were denouncing the calumniators of the guillotine. Hébert was still loud-mouthed, but Paris was hungry in the winter, and for some

[343]

strange reason it held Hébert responsible. In March, Robespierre was strong enough to order his arrest, and, with other members of the Commune, he was guillotined almost without a public protest, and the Commune ceased to function.

At once the Committee moved against Danton and Desmoulins. Its policy was the policy of the Russian Bolshevists—to suppress all opposition both from the Right and from the Left. It was Saint-Just, "the archangel of death," who denounced Danton in the Convention from notes supplied by Robespierre. He had been ill and continually absent from the Committee, but he specifically and deliberately consented to the trial and to the certain conviction. It is the death of Danton that has branded Robespierre with undying infamy, and the infamy has become more coloured because Danton was a great Titan of a man, magnificent in his virtues and his vices, while Robespierre was a drab precisian, mean both in virtue and in vice. Danton lived finely and died finely, with a masculine humour rarely paralleled in the annals of man. "If I could leave my legs to Couthon," he said one

[344]

day in his prison, "and my virility to Robespierre, things might still go on." There is a touch of the theatrical in: "I am Danton, not unknown among the revolutionaries. I shall be living nowhere soon, but you will find my name in Valhalla." But there is great and proper pride in the last words: "Show my head to the people. It is well worth while."

Danton dead, Robespierre was the Republic, and the Republic was for the moment triumphant. But not for long. On May 12th, the day of Danton's death, when he stayed behind the curtains, pale-faced, trembling, and for the first time perhaps doubting his formula, and perhaps, too, doubting for himself, he can hardly have guessed that he had a bare eleven weeks to live.

Robespierre's Republic was triumphant, and Robespierre's Republic must have a god—not the God of the Catholic Church, incalculable, not to be measured, hardly to be explained, but a Supreme Being made in the likeness of the lawyer of Arras. Five days before the execution of Danton he read to the Convention a long and tedious report on religion and morals, and the Convention passed a decree containing the two clauses:

1. The French people recognise the existence of the Supreme Being and the immortality of the soul.
2. They acknowledge that the worship of the Supreme Being is one of the duties of man.

The speech contained one fine truth in the assertion that atheism is aristocratic. It contained, too, the often-quoted political axiom, "If God did not exist, it would be necessary to invent Him." The nature of Robespierre's God derives from the pages of Rousseau, and is explained in the passage: "The true priest of the Supreme Being is nature; His temple the universe; His religion virtue; His fêtes the joy of a great people assembled under His eyes to draw closer the sweet bonds of universal fraternity and to present to Him the homage of pure and sensitive souls."

At first docile Paris accepted Robespierre's God as it had accepted Hébert's blasphemies, but Paris was soon bored. The new worship was launched on June 8th on the Champ de Mars, Robespierre, as always neat and clean in his attire, carrying a cardboard statue of atheism in the procession, which was subsequently burned amid the plaudits of the people.

Having re-established God, Robespierre tightened up the revolutionary tribunal. Prisoners were no longer to be permitted to defend themselves. And now, as he thought, having suppressed all possible opponents, he proceeded to make the tragic blunder that hurried his life to an end. Robespierre triumphant showed himself the true Robespierre, the Puritan Robespierre. At the end of May he arrested Tallien's mistress, afterwards to be his wife—"the round beautiful woman, daughter of Cabarus the Spanish merchant, whom fox-haired Tallien had met while massacring in Bordeaux," as Carlyle describes her. It was the men without principle, without morals, without ideals, that Robespierre was now determined to suppress, and it was these mean men—Tallien, Fouché, Barrère—who were to be the executioners of him who had sent the heads of great men into Samson's basket.

There were plottings, secret meetings, hesitations. Carnot was too busy with his armies to care much about political intrigue. Barrère hesitated. The Gascon adventurer had once described Robespierre as "a pigmy who should not be seated on a pedestal," but he afterwards became his henchman. He was a man of no scruples and some power of oratory, and he is remembered best for the mouthing statement, "The tree of liberty could not grow were it not watered with the blood of kings." He lived till 1841, to be a pensioner of Louis Philippe. Tallien, fearful for his wife, and Fouché, fearful for himself, were the most formidable of the plotters.

At last the stage was set for the 9th Thermidor (July 27th, 1794). It was a dull and stormy morning. Robespierre's enemies and his friends had been up all night preparing accusation and defence. But he slept soundly, dressed in the morning with his usual neatness in a light blue coat, and said a genial good-bye to the anxious Duplays. It was twelve o'clock when he reached the Convention. Tallien, Fouché, Barrère, were sitting together, not a little apprehensive. The debate was irrelevant, disorderly, inchoate. Saint-Just was interrupted. Tallien, ever the second-rate actor, brandished a dagger and declared his determination to stab the tyrant. Barrère tried to arrive at some sort of compromise. And it was late in the afternoon when there occurred the final scene, described with broad and effective dramatic power by Carlyle and with meticulous care by Mr. Belloc. Robespierre's first intervention worked his undoing. Tallien had shouted that the discussion must be brought back to the point, and Robespierre angrily commented, "I shall know well enough how to bring back the debate to order." It was a blunt, inopportune declaration of personal authority. It was greeted with loud and repeated shouts of "Tyrant," which continued when Robespierre had mounted the tribune, standing there hesitating, spluttering, without self-control or dignity, while an unknown deputy gibed at him with "The blood of Danton is choking you." His arrest was ordered. His two friends Couthon and Saint-Just, and his brother, Augustin, were arrested with him, though for a while the police were too startled and terrified to lay hands on them. Robespierre was stunned. His end had come so swiftly, so unexpectedly. In the last days of his life he appears more bloodless, insensitive, inhuman than ever. His jaw was broken by a bullet fired by a nineteen-years-old boy, and the precise dandy went to his death with a filthy bandage on his head. Women cursed him as he mounted the scaffold, still insensible, still bewildered. But there were bitter tears for him in the house of the Duplays, and Saint-Just, who died for love of him, was among the fine revolutionary figures. With Robespierre the Revolution came to an end. France was prepared for the Napoleonic drama after the brief immoral posturings of the Directoire.

Mr. Belloc suggests that Robespierre was probably far greater than he seemed. Fate had cast him for a great part in one of the greatest world dramas, and he played it meanly; but, as Carlyle has said, "He was a man fitted in some luckier settled age to have been one of those incorruptible barren Pattern-Figures, and have had marble tablets and funeral sermons." He was universally recognised as honest and incorruptible. Fortunes were made out of the sales of national estates. Robespierre made nothing. Comfortable, well-paid positions were secured by the most vehement of the Jacobins. Robespierre continued to lead his simple life with the Duplays. He had a narrow political faith, but he was unswervingly true to his faith.

He would indeed have been almost certain of comfortable and somewhat priggish eminence in Victorian England.

THE END